FIVE MEN ONE LOAF

A Gwent soldier's tale
by Haden Spicer

Running Heads

RUNNING HEADS PUBLISHING

9 Frederick Place, Clifton, Bristol BS8 1AS

First published 1990

ISBN: 0 9516344 0 2

British library cataloguing in publication data
Spicer, Haden 1923
Five men one loaf: A Gwent soldier's tale
1. France and Germany. British Prisoners of War, 1939–45
Title 940.54724 3092

Designed by Kurt Stengel for Blue Sax
Typesetting by PCS Typesetting, Frome, Somerset
Printed by View Publications, Wickwar, Gloucestershire
Set in 11/12½ Bembo

FIVE MEN ONE LOAF

Chapter one

We were lying in a ditch in Normandy in the outskirts of Mouen, a hamlet near Mondrainville, a village a few miles south of Caen, foot-soldiers, taking cover from German mortar fire. There were a dozen or so of us scattered along a fifty-yard stretch. The rest of the platoon had just returned from a patrol, bringing back long French loaves and eggs, some of which they had given to the platoon commander, a Canadian. He began to share the food out, so I crawled up the ditch for my share. When I reached him it seemed that he had been waiting for me, because instead of handing me some bread he surprised me by asking me to go forward to the farmhouse about fifty yards ahead of us, to see if I could brew up some tea for the platoon. I suppose he detailed me because he knew that I could speak some schoolboy French. The noise of the mortar explosions had increased even as I crawled up the ditch, so I told him that I didn't fancy the idea at all and particularly not on my own. He detailed another man to go with me, which rather spiked my guns and clutching my gun in one hand and a large tin of ready mixed tea, sugar and dried milk in the other, off we set.

We crawled along the ditch until we came to the end of the field. We turned at right angles alongside one of the impenetrable Normandy hedges behind which was a long barn, and moved along until we came to a five barred gate which was the entrance to the large yard in front of the farmhouse. Looking through the lower part of the gate we could see that the farmyard, though large, was fully paved, with the odd farming implement dotted about and with a row of hutches containing rabbits along the wall farthest from us. We naturally reasoned that a door to the house must lead off from the farmyard, so when the mortar fire eased off a little we very quickly shinned over the gate and dashed around to the front of the building to find the door we had expected, which luckily was wide open. We rushed inside to find ourselves in a small hallway, at the foot of a flight of wooden stairs, with a large room off to the right which we went straight into to find ourselves in the kitchen.

The farmhouse must have been very old, with its great thick walls, and seated around the room on the floor with their backs against the walls were an oldish man, probably the farmer, and three or four women in black dresses, obviously trying to get some protection from the mortar fire. A fire was burning in a wood stove and gesturing vaguely at it I went down the kitchen. On a table near the stove I found a large two-handled aluminium pan already three quarters full of water, which I put on the stove. I stoked the fire up a bit and waited for the water to boil.

The water heated very quickly and as it started to come to the boil I put my gun on the kitchen table, took out my clasp knife and opened the tin of ready mixed "tea". I was just going to tip the mixture into the water when out of the corner of my eye I noticed movement from beneath the open window which faced onto the farmyard. One of the young French women in her long black dress had got up from the floor where she was sheltering. She quickly came down the kitchen towards me, caught hold of me by the shoulder, turned me towards the window and said, in a voice that was hoping I would understand, *"Kamerad, Boche!"* without the slightest trace of fear.

My mind was still on tea-making but I came to with a start as I looked in the direction she was pointing and saw a German patrol cautiously spreading out across the farmyard. The brave girl must have heard them through the open window. Feeling trapped I snatched up my gun and looked for a way out. The only door was the one which let onto the hallway with the wide open front door. The only windows were the ones which looked out on the farmyard. There were no windows at the back of the kitchen so if we wanted to get away we would have to go upstairs. The bare wooden steps of the stairway in the small hall were immediately in front of the open front door. We stood cautiously in the kitchen doorway for a while before I motioned for my companion to make a dash for it up the stairs. As he rushed up he was spotted by the enemy, so that as I followed him up a few minutes later they opened fire. As I ran up bullets tore holes in the wood below my heels. At the top the stairs turned sharp left onto a small landing with an open window which looked down on the farmyard. My companion on reaching the landing had fired through the open window and then ducked away, so that as I arrived at the top of the stairs, with the bottom of the open window facing me at waist height, a hail of bullets whistled around my ears as the Germans fired back. I dodged very quickly into a bedroom on my left. The open window of the room looked down into the farmyard. I stood back from it and looked out warily to see nine or ten jackbooted, grey-green uniformed, helmeted, heavily-armed Germans dotted about, taking whatever little cover there was. I moved forward, took aim and fired a long burst at the ones most in view and then my Sten gun jammed. As I feverishly tried to clear the gun, sweat ran into my eyes so that I could not see, and for a long moment I stupidly stood at the open window before coming to my senses and hastily moving to one side.

The noise of my burst of machine-gun fire must have reverberated through the house, because from downstairs came the shrieks and screams of the French family as I continued to try to get my jammed machine gun working again. After a while the house became very quiet and then I heard German voices from the kitchen below. The enemy had got into the house, and I had to get away somehow.

Thinking that the Germans might start shooting through the ceilings, knowing that we were upstairs, I moved and stood with my back against the wall, as I looked for a way out of our predicament. I could see that the bedroom I was in was the same as the kitchen – the only window was the one I had fired through, facing the farmyard, so there was no way out through this room. I had to look further, so very quickly I inched my way along the wall, ducked beneath the open window, and crawled along the landing. I got into another bedroom on the right, where I found that my companion had taken cover. This was the master bedroom with a large bed which was covered with newspapers on which were mounds of yellow butter, most peculiar I thought as I looked around, only to find that this room too held no means of escape, with its only window looking out onto the farmyard.

It began to look as if we were definitely trapped, but looking further around we discovered a narrow flight of stone stairs which were part of the dividing wall of the house. We clambered up there to find ourselves in the attics and there, set in the thick wall at the back of the house, was a narrow Norman arched opening with rusted cross-shaped iron bars. In desperation I lifted my foot and kicked hard at the bars, which to my intense relief fell out into the field below. Without any hesitation, and not even bothering to look down, I squeezed through the narrow opening, jumped, and was running before I hit the ground.

I landed heavily in a field alongside a hedge on my left hand side, which was a barrier between me and the comrades whom I had left behind in the ditch. The hedge was typical of those in Normandy at that time. It had not been trimmed for years and was thick and almost impenetrable with an earth mound at the base. As I ran like mad along it I searched for a way through to enable me to rejoin my platoon. Suddenly, I became aware of noises like bees buzzing around me. Surprisingly I heard no sound of gunfire, and then I realised that I was being shot at from all sides. It was not, as I had thought, just a German patrol in the farmyard, but quite a large force making a counter-attack and I was running right across its front.

Then I felt a peculiar sensation in my left arm and the gun I was carrying fell from my grasp. I let out a great shout and burst straight through the, until then, impenetrable hedge and threw myself to the ground. Not wanting to be pinpointed I crawled as flat as possible away from where I had first taken cover behind the mound of earth at the bottom of the hedge. I kept moving along until I reached a fold in the ground under the hedge, which seemed to afford some protection, and there I stopped to take stock of my situation.

I had been shot in the fleshy part of the arm just below the elbow. The sleeve of my battledress was already sodden with blood, but I felt very little pain. I lay close to the ground, panting and getting my breath back, when I heard German voices from the other side of the hedge. I clung even closer to the ground, keeping still as a mouse.

It was a lovely morning at the end of June. I could hear birds singing and the herd of black and white cows in the field with me had settled down to munching the long grass after being disturbed by the gunfire. As I lay there, thinking of how I could get back to my comrades, I heard the sound of running footsteps coming towards me. I twisted my head around to see my companion from the farmhouse flinging himself on the ground next to me. Getting his breath back he asked whether I had been hit. I told him that I had, and I realised that my left arm was in something of a mess and that the ground where I was lying was becoming soaked with my blood.

My companion had given my position away and was restless to make a move by running for it. I warned him that there were Germans on the other side of the hedge we were sheltering behind. I wished I had not said anything, because with an instinctive reaction he raised himself up and said "Where?" A single shot rang out and he collapsed beside me with the breath gushing out of him.

As I twisted around still further, to see what had happened to him, I noticed movement near the long barn along which we had crawled to get to the farmhouse. The barn had a large opening high in the wall for moving bales of hay and the like in and out, and after a while I saw a German machine gun crew setting up their Spandau in the opening, which gave them a clear field of fire right down the ditch. Suddenly, from the ditch, a Bren gun opened up. The bullets raked the wall of the barn to the left of the opening, moved slowly across and then concentrated on the German gunners who were hurled backwards.

This was the signal for all hell to break loose and I was lying right in the middle of it. Machine guns from both sides fired incessantly for what seemed like hours, with bullets flying over my head from all directions. When there was the occasional lull the rumble of tanks was clearly audible. The machine gun fire finally died down and then an artillery barrage started up. It sounded as if shells were coming from British twenty-five pounders which were laying a curtain of fire all around me. Shells began to fall in the field where I was taking cover and the herd of cows went mad. Several were hit by shrapnel as they charged round the field in sheer terror, frightening me more than the shellfire. As the bombardment went on I was raised off the ground by explosions and dropped back hard. I was getting weak from loss of blood, the shellfire was getting heavier and things were becoming hazy. I suppose I must have passed out.

Chapter two

I came to rather dopily to find myself being kicked in the ribs by a tall helmeted German with a half moon shaped medallion on his chest, hanging from a chain around his neck. He was pointing a sub-machine gun at me. When I stirred he motioned me to my feet with his gun. I stood up and he turned over my motionless companion with a jackbooted foot. My companion had been shot in the head just below his left eye. Lying on the ground, on his face, had trapped the wound, and when he was roughly turned the blood gushed out in a spout from the hole. The German then turned to me and motioned for me to hold my hands over my head before starting to search me thoroughly. I was carrying my spare Sten gun magazines in the large pocket on the front of my battledress trousers. These he quickly found, took them out, looked them over and then flung them away. Next he found my tin of "iron rations" in my back pocket. This he opened, liked what he saw and pocketed it. Then, continuing his search, he came across my first aid bandage, a field dressing which I was carrying in the small pocket of my trousers and pocketed it straightaway.

He obviously knew what he was after, because he then gave me a quick checkover, looked me hard in the face and said in quite good English, as if he had done the same thing many times before, "For you the war is over".

All was peaceful and quiet, the sun was still shining as he motioned me to move along the hedge towards an opening out of the field away from the farmhouse, while he followed about ten paces behind with his gun trained on me. As I came through the opening into a grassy lane alongside a railway line, my one arm raised higher than the other, German infantry popped up from the sides of the lane and raised their levelled rifles at me. I thought that it was the end of me, because I didn't know who was the most startled, but my captor appeared in sight behind me and the guns were lowered. He motioned for me to turn right into the lane, marched me for about twenty yards and then signalled for me to get into a deep ditch to join a German infantryman. No sooner had I dropped into the ditch than the bombardment started up again and machine guns started hammering away. The German and I cowered in the bottom of the ditch which seemed to be a company headquarters, because a German officer with a field telephone appeared to be directing operations from there, with his binoculars searching out ahead whenever the shelling ceased.

The ditch was so narrow that the German and I sat with our backs against one side of it with our knees bent up under our chins, shoulder to shoulder, showing no signs of enmity in the dangerous situation, so much so that he started to talk to me in broken English. He was as young as me, an Austrian, and he pulled a photograph of a young woman out of his pocket, telling me that she was his girlfriend. She looked an old fashioned type to me so I responded by getting out of my battledress pocket the photograph of my girl and we held them side by side in comparison. I must admit I didn't think a lot of his, but I certainly wasn't going to say anything. Being so close together I noticed the difference in the uniforms we were wearing. He was dressed in the grey-green jacket and trousers of the German army, both of which were quite threadbare, and his feet were shod not in jackboots but in ordinary boots that were quite down at heel. My uniform, apart from the bloodstains,was brand new in contrast, a whitish khaki from the anti-louse powder with which it had been compressed, and the rest of my clothing was new as well. Some months before the invasion we had been measured and fitted out completely with new gear which we had tried on for size. We then handed it back into the company stores to await reissue a few days before we actually moved out of Aldershot on our way to the coast. It was all so new that the anti-louse powder had hardly had time to get worn off, whereas the Austrian's uniform didn't look as serviceable as my second best battledress back in England.

During one lull in the shooting another British prisoner was pushed into the ditch with us. He took one look at my bloodstained sleeve and offered to do something for me. I was very grateful for this, because my arm was becoming stiff and painful. While the shells were dropping all around us he took out his clasp knife, which funnily enough hadn't been taken away from him, and started sawing at my clothes. He cut the sleeve of my battledress jacket off above the elbow and slid it downwards off my arm. Then he did the same with my long sleeved pullover and my shirt, each piece of clothing looking like a piece of liver with its thick layer of congealed blood.

The bullet which hit me had passed clean through the fleshy part of my arm, just below the elbow, but luckily not damaging any bones, in at the front of my arm and out at the back. After I had been shot my sleeves must have moved and covered the holes and, as my arm swelled, must have stopped some of the blood escaping. That, coupled with internal bleeding, meant that my arm contained a lot of loose blood. This was causing the arm and even my fingers to swell up, and in time they looked like black pudding, with congealed blood from my shoulder to my fingertips lying below the surface of the skin.

Although my initial captor had taken my field dressing from the pocket of my trousers, I had another one in the inside pocket of my battledress jacket, which luckily he had missed. My captive companion fished this out and carefully bandaged me up. My left arm was now bare from the elbow down except for the bandage, and this bareness was something I was going to regret in the long cold nights ahead.

During another lull in the action a most peculiar captive was put in the ditch. He was dressed as if he were going out to a dance on a Saturday night. He wore a collar and tie under an immaculate battledress, black civilian shoes and a Scottish cap perched on top of his bespectacled face — a cap with a chequered band around it and black ribbons hanging down at the back. His whole appearance looked unreal to me until he explained that he was the driver of a Naafi truck who had lost his way and didn't realise that he was in enemy territory until a bullet hole appeared in the truck's windscreen and he found himself surrounded by Germans. Somehow we were wary of him because of his appearance and more particularly when he began to make suggestions about escaping. Either he was a fraud or he genuinely didn't appreciate that he had landed up in the middle of a battle with the German army.

By late afternoon all was quiet again and then we were motioned out of the ditch to be accompanied to the rear by two walking wounded

German infantrymen. They had been cut in the legs by the look of it and as they walked along their bandages came undone and trailed behind them from their trouser legs. The amazing thing was that the bandages were made of paper which made me understand why my captor had been so keen to get his hands on a British field dressing.

The sun was still shining as we made our way through a long sloping field of corn dotted with the single foxholes of German infantrymen who occasionally popped up like rabbits to have a look at us. The cornfield lay alongside a railway line and as we passed a large deep cutting we saw long columns of German infantry taking cover against the sides.

Finally we came to the end of the field and dropped down into a lane alongside a red brick wall. We came face to face with a blond haired, blue eyed German officer witn polished jackboots, brand new binoculars and map case hanging from leather straps around his neck and with a revolver in a highly polished holster at his side. With an imperious gesture he stopped us and began to go through our pockets. As he came to each item, paybook, letters from home, photographs of girlfriends, occupation money, he didn't bother to look at them but tossed them, with a theatrical gesture, high in the air and over the wall. It looked to me as if he were not right in the head and I couldn't help a little smile creeping onto my features. Unfortunately he noticed my reaction. He went berserk, almost started frothing at the mouth and began to scrabble at his revolver holster. Luckily the two German front line soldiers accompanying us pushed us away and rushed us down the lane. We kept walking for some time until we came to a wide main road, uninhabited except for the odd villa type house dotted here and there. Everywhere seemed completely deserted and very quiet except for the noise of our boots on the tarmac. We seemed to be moving in a lost world when ahead of us we heard and saw a large tank coming down the road towards us. As it did so, from the distance came the drone of an aircraft. The occupants of the tank, who must have been keeping a very keen lookout overhead, spotted it as a small speck. Suddenly the tank did an abrupt right turn and smashed into one of the small detached houses just off the road, which totally collapsed in a great cloud of dust, completely hiding the tank from view. The aeroplane sheered off in another direction while we stood there fascinated until ordered to march on down the road.

The reaction of the German tank crew surprised us because we had never been harassed by German aircraft except for a pair of single engined fighters, probably Messerschmidts, which came over our positions one day, hedge-hopping about fifty feet from the ground. We could see the pilots clearly as they slowly flew over with the rear aeroplane offset at an angle from the front one. We had not been particularly afraid of them so it seemed that the Allied forces must have had complete air superiority. Eventually we reached a large orchard. This was some sort of headquarters with large areas of camouflage netting spread across the tops of the trees to increase the cover. There was also a large cooking area with German cooks busily preparing food on field kitchens. Here my companion and I were separated and I was seated under a tree among the cooks who were, I presumed, supposed to keep an eye on me. I was left alone to gather my thoughts. The shame of being taken prisoner slowly came over me. Only that morning I had been a member of a proud fighting unit and now here I was in captivity.

I was in the orchard for hours and my mind kept turning over the fact that all the time and preparation I had been through in readiness for the invasion of Europe had completely evaporated in one summer's afternoon. In a way, I suppose I was lucky to be alive. Some of this was no doubt due to the intensive training I had been through, not least in house to house fighting which must have helped me to keep cool when we were trapped in the farmhouse.

This training had taken place in London. We had been trucked down from Yorkshire to billets in Ilford where we stayed for a week in empty houses in a long terraced row. We slept on the bare floorboards at the end of winter, in cold damp rooms, so that we were glad to get out in the early morning to be trucked to the training course. This was in the East End of London near the docks, where a large area had been flattened by German bombers during the Blitz. The place was so big that live ammunition could be used without fear of harming anyone. Most of the houses had been totally destroyed but there were some partially standing in the midst of the rubble, which we used to play hide and seek in a warlike manner. We learned to fight and conceal ourselves in the debris and how to flush out the enemy. Some of this training must have rubbed off on me to enable me to escape from the farmhouse, so it wasn't all wasted, but I couldn't help thinking about the vast amount of other forms of training that I had been through. At the time I didn't think so, but it's not so much the actual shooting that a footsoldier does, but his mere presence on the ground, that helps to win battles. Somebody has to occupy the ground, and it can really only be done by infantry. Training to sleep rough, to march tirelessly for mile after mile, to be fit and strong, to occupy the ground no matter what the weather, all this had no doubt accomplished something in Normandy, so I must have made some contribution, but I still couldn't help thinking what a waste it all was. I had definitely had visions of myself as a "Death or Glory" boy when we set sail from England, and instead here I was, a prisoner of war.

I felt very miserable, and must have looked it, so that when the time came to move on, one of the cooks offered me a whole loaf of bread. I refused, although it was obviously a goodwill gesture, and I hadn't eaten since the previous day. It was almost as if by accepting it I was also accepting the reality of my situation. I was to think about that refused loaf many times in the days ahead, because it heralded the start of days without food of any description.

Chapter three

Another prisoner was brought along and we were both put into an open staff car with a driver and two armed guards. One sat in the folded roof cover of the car, unceasingly scanning the skies. The other couldn't help glancing nervously upwards either. All three were extremely nervous and jumpy and as we raced along the country roads we soon saw the reason why. The roadsides were littered with the debris of burnt out cars, lorries, ruined carts and dead horses. Here and there, usually where there were the remains of several vehicles in one place, were the graves of German soldiers marked with crosses. It seemed that the three Germans had every right to be scared of the Allied airforces.

The sight of so many horses and carts still being used by the Germans came as something of a surprise. I'd always thought of the German army as being highly mechanised after reading of their Blitzkrieg tactics when they overran Europe. The effect of their Tiger tanks on our Armoured Division Shermans had made me think that their equipment was far superior to ours, but here they were obviously relying quite heavily on horsedrawn transport, something which the Allied armies had long ago forsaken. The only time I had seen Army horses was once when we were being lorried through a small town in Yorkshire and passed a regimental barracks. There on a yellow gravelled driveway stood a cart drawn by a well-groomed horse with its driver standing alongside. It obviously had a traditional antiquated function which, like rubber-necked tourists, we found intriguing.

We eventually reached a small cluster of cottages in the middle of nowhere, where the car pulled up and we were ordered out. As we got out a small crowd of French women appeared, gathered around us and started to give the "V" for victory sign with their two fingers raised. They gasped sorrowfully and some had tears in their eyes when they saw my bloodstained battledress jacket with its sawn-off sleeve and my bandaged arm. I couldn't understand how the women could be so brave in front of such heavily-armed German soldiers. I was too nervous even to acknowledge their signals in the face of the growing hostility of the guards. As we were making our way through the crowd there was a sudden panic as a low flying plane shot over the top of us. As it wheeled around we were pushed by a guard into the nearest cottage. Here were two old French peasants, a man and his wife by the look of it, who were just sitting down at a bare topped wooden table to a bowl of soup and pieces of bread. When we were pushed into the small room the guard roughly shoved them up against one wall and lined us up against another. Then he stood in the middle of the room listening intently as the plane roared low over the top of the cottage. He stood stock still until the engine noise faded away in the distance.

After a while we were taken out and stood outside another cottage where we were taken inside one at a time to be interrogated. The room the interrogator was in had been blacked out so that he could hardly be seen, but what could not be missed was the large pistol on the table in front of him, which he lifted threateningly when his questions drew a blank. Not that I was being brave but I honestly didn't know any of the answers. For example I had no idea of the name of the place where I had been captured, and he had great difficulty in believing this. There had never been any training or discussion back in England about the possibility of being taken prisoner. It had never entered our heads that it might happen to us and certainly as far as regiments were concerned, they didn't want to know about the matter. Regiments were only too proud to report that in an engagement so many were killed and that no-one was taken prisoner - fighting to the last man was what regiments wanted to hear about. So we only had vague recollections about the fact that we were only required to give our number, name and rank to a captor.

This vague notion about number, rank and name made one assume that one would be questioned in a tidy way, but the darkened room and the levelled pistol were frightening, which they were meant to be, and I was very glad to get out into the open again after the interrogator summarily dismissed me.

The whole thing was over in a matter of minutes and we were shoved back into the staff car to be driven off with darkness falling to arrive at a large country house. We were put into a windowless room where we met up with a motley bunch of prisoners from different regiments and the door was locked behind us. Looking around us we saw that one of the occupants was a major from a tank regiment, obviously a Middle East veteran with a spotted silk scarf around his neck, suede boots and black beret. He kept himself well aloof from the rest of us and was obviously not at all happy with the company he was forced to keep.

Another occupant was a Canadian who told us that he was a sniper who had been hiding for three days in a cupboard in a house that had been retaken and occupied by the Germans. They would not have found him but he had to give himself up because of thirst. The three days had had an ill effect on him as was evidenced by his jumpy manner and a strange white pallor under the black stubble on his face.

There were a few other odd individuals there, all from different regiments, looking completely lost and bemused and I sat down next to one of them on the wooden floor. As it grew darker he told me that his name was George and that he had been a gunner in a Churchill tank that had been converted to a flame thrower. Now the Germans hated flame throwers and invariably shot anyone connected with them. George's tank was in a squadron of three that attacked a wood containing German infantrymen. As they were withdrawing they lost a track and were immobilised.The other two tanks stayed with them until darkness fell, although they were surrounded by enemy infantry, but then had to leave them to return to the safety of their tank laager. As the night wore on the crew could hear the Germans outside and realising that they were about to be blown up, decided to surrender. They climbed out of the tank one by one, were lined up against its side and all killed except for George, for some inexplicable reason.

George was about my age and we became quite friendly as we recounted our experiences of the day to one another.

It was the time of the year when days are at their longest. It had been a very long, hard day for all of us. Worn out and exhausted, we fell asleep on the bare wooden boards of our prison.

The next morning we were rudely awakened by loud shouting, cleared out of the room, pushed into a lorry and driven for some miles, with the guards anxiously scanning the skies. We eventually arrived at a large horse-riding establishment which had been taken over by the Germans for use as a temporary prison because of the high walls which surrounded it. Here we met up with a large number of prisoners of all nationalities.

There was a cold water tap in the outside yard of the complex, so I carefully teased the bandage off my arm and inspected the wound. The arm was very swollen, and the loose blood under the skin had started to blacken, as had the congealed blood in my fingers which had swollen to twice their normal size. The field dressing was stiff with blood so I washed it out under the tap. When it was clean, George re-wrapped it around the wound.

We spent the rest of the day hoping that we might get something to eat but nothing came forth and when night fell we moved inside to a riding hall with a thick layer of peat on its floor on which we laid our heads. We soon fell asleep on our soft bed, although it was rather smelly due to the horse manure which was well mixed with the peat.

Morning came and we were pushed out into the open yard, counted a couple of times and then driven off in lorries to the outskirts of Alençon. Here was the first taste of a prisoner of war camp. It was said that the large huts, enclosed with barbed wire, into which we were escorted, had been used as a prison camp in the First World War, and were once again being used for that purpose.

There were hundreds of prisoners already there and for the first time I came into direct contact with Americans, most of whom had come from the bloody battle for St. Lô. There were also some of the men from my company, that I had crawled away from. They told me that they had been overwhelmed and that most of my closest comrades were dead.

These men from my company formed a tight little group. Funnily enough I didn't join them but I tended to stick with George. This was something that seemed to happen to most people - the tendency was to stick with those first encountered when you were taken prisoner. Also, I had never been very friendly with most of the men in my new battalion to which I had been transferred about a year before the invasion, but had chummed up and stayed that way with another new recruit to the battalion who had joined them at about the same time as me. It had been a territorial battalion before the war started, when the men had been mobilised, and consequently they tended to be somewhat older than we two. They were also in very tight groups, had been together for a very long time and came from the same close neighbourhoods.

My friend of the same age was in the same platoon as I but in a different section. I'd lost his company early on because he had been left behind in reserve when we were moved forward to the battlefront, so at least he had missed the misfortune of the rest of us. Leaving men behind in reserve at various stages was something we had not been prepared for and we thought that it tended to ruin the efficiency of the various units of the battalion. The platoon sergeant had also been left behind as we moved up and his place had been taken by a corporal, a section leader. This meant that even I had been made a section leader the day before the massacre. The trouble was that we had had no training at all for this situation: one result was a small breakdown of discipline.

The shedding of various members of the battalion had started in Aldershot just before our move nearer to the South Coast. Men who, in my eyes, had always had all the "perks" that were going, and were always well looked after, suddenly disappeared for a variety of reasons, such as having a low grade of fitness, and the battalion became very trimmed down in numbers. Now that the time had come to face serious action, the ones who had always had the best of things in the battalion, had been the blue-eyed boys, were out of it, and the rifle-carrying footsloggers were becoming increasingly isolated.

When we did finally leave Aldershot a quota of fighting men was kept back in reserve. When even more were held back in Normandy we began to realise how much of a sharp end of the army we really were. A rifle-carrying footsoldier is very much at the apex of a pyramid with all the various supporting functions beneath him. Sometimes it felt lonely that way, so that I really had very little inclination to join in with the newcomers from the battalion.

Odd prisoners were escorted into the compound at various times. One of them turned out to be the Company Sergeant-Major, whom I must say I wasn't too pleased to see because of the way he had treated me back in England. He was quite old for an infantryman and I was surprised that he had come to Normandy with us.

When we were stationed in Yorkshire most of our time was spent in military exercises, which meant that from Monday to Friday we were out in the open countryside of the Yorkshire moors, sleeping rough. We worked as sections with a corporal in charge, who was about the only non-commissioned officer we ever came into contact with. This meant that very few people were ever charged with disciplinary offences, so there was a dearth of people sentenced to carry out the many dirty tasks which needed doing in and around an infantry battalion.

I'm sure that this dearth was the reason for the battalion drill parade which was held on Saturday mornings, an idea which no doubt was thought up in conspiracy by the senior Sergeant-Majors. We were stationed in Hornsea at the time, sleeping on the bare floorboards of unoccupied houses just off the seafront when we were not out in the countryside. The drill parade was taken by the Regimental Sergeant-Major on the promenade in all winds and weathers. He stood on a raised area and the rest of us with our backs to the sea and non-commissioned officers behind us. As many people as possible contrived to get off this parade, and so it usually consisted of the rifle sections only, about three hundred of us.

The first part of the parade was supposed to consist of getting the whole battalion in a column of threes graded from the tallest at both ends to the shortest in the middle. This exercise usually took up the whole of the morning and quite often did not get completed, because it was quite a complicated procedure with so many men. If it had been explained to us what they were trying to do then it would probably have been executed quite smartly, but this would have destroyed the devious reason for the whole operation, namely to get a large number of men on disciplinary charges and sentenced to carry out the dirty fatigues which were mounting up.

We were all aware that the whole procedure was fraught with the danger of having one's name taken and thus having a sentence passed, and there were many hazards to be overcome. The first was that invariably the wind came off the sea. This meant that the RSM's voice was blown back to him and was inaudible at each end of the parade. So in the first instance, while waiting for the parade to start, it was worthwhile to get in the area in front of him, although it was dangerous in itself to be under his beady eye, because after each shouted instruction the words "Take that man's name, Corporal!" invariably followed. "Battalion! Battalion! Atten-shun" started the proceedings, and those few at the very ends of the line who were slow in responding duly had their names taken. A corporal would fall in as a marker and then came, "Tallest on the left, shortest on the right, fall in !"

This caused a lot of pushing and shoving but very few names were taken, except for those unlucky enough to give vent to their feelings out loud, whereupon the RSM's voice would scream out, "Take that man's name, Corporal, that man next to the man with ginger hair, talking!"

One wondered how he could hear so well, but of course the wind was invariably off the sea blowing any sound towards him, and also the NCOs behind us were probably raising their hands and pointing out culprits for him.

The next, "Battalion! Right dress!" and we would raise our right arms to touch the shoulder of the man on our right, pointing our heads to the right and with much shuffling about get into a well-spaced straight line of three hundred men, which stretched for quite a distance down the promenade.

When everything had settled down and silence had fallen, the next screamed order came: "Battalion, by the left, number!" and off we would go ... "One, two, three, four...", but on a windy day it was difficult to hear what the man on the left had said, particularly if he had a quiet voice or a North Wales accent. There was no pause in the numbering, so any old number which was about right was shouted out in a strangulated voice. This misnumbering was passed on down the whole of the line, and it took its toll in the next operation, which was when the fun really started.

There was usually a gap in the shouted orders now, as we stood in one long line stiffly to attention, not daring to move a muscle or utter a word. Then it would come - "Battalion! Odd numbers one pace forward, even numbers one pace back, March!"

Some men would have forgotten the number they had shouted out, others had shouted the wrong number in any case. There were even those who didn't know what was meant by the words "odd and even numbers". So instead of two well-spaced lines of men two paces apart, there would be many instances of two or even three together in the front and a great gap in the new line. As realisation dawned, men would start shuffling backwards or forwards, desperately trying to put things right, resulting in a complete and utter shambles. "Take their names!" would resound along the promenade and the corporals would have a field day. The only thing to do was to stand stiffly to attention and stare unseeingly to the front, even if you were wrong in the first instance, and hope that you would be ignored. The chaos resulting from this manoeuvre was so bad that the whole parade was usually fallen out, and we would start all over again.

When we did finally master the drill up to this point, there were yet further hazards. After we were in two spaced out orderly lines the next order was "Battalion - ranks, right and left turn!"

This was supposed to mean that the front rank turned to the left, and the rear rank to the right, but not until we had tried it a few times did the message sink in. That is, if the men at the ends of the line heard the order at all when the wind was brisk, and the RSM was not above lowering his voice to make things more difficult, particularly if the catch of men on charges was low.

Then came the final order, to march forward and fall in in column of threes, which should have resulted in a tidy parade with the tallest men on the ends tapering down to the shortest in the middle. The whole battalion would move forward in step at quite a sharp pace and come to a halt in columns of threes, with NCOs trying their best to guide men into the correct place. The slightest hiccup with the whole battalion moving forward, and yet another shambles would ensue.

This drill went on for many Saturdays with a lot of men on fatigues as a result of having had their names taken. But then one day it all went right, with the wind coming from inland, nobody speaking a word, and the sun shining. The parade was so successful that we were marched up and down the promenade and very few names were taken.

This augured ill for other opportunities to be put on a charge, and was where I fell down. On the following Monday morning the first parade was for physical training, at about seven in the morning, where we turned out in white PT vest and blue shorts. Over the weekends, in the evenings, when we were allowed out, the smart gear was to wear the white PT vest back to front with the battledress neck undone so that the white vest showed over the top of the shirt. Having only two PT vests, one was in the laundry and on checking on Sunday evening I found that the one I had been wearing as "smart gear" was decidedly grubby. I washed it out and hung it to dry indoors. The weather was bad, damp and dull, so that when I came to put the vest on, early on Monday morning, I found that it was still soaking wet. As I slipped it on I hoped that the warmth of my body would dry it out, but when we fell in for the PT parade it was still very wet.

As we stood there the Company Sergeant-Major appeared and started to inspect us, accompanied by a corporal. On reaching me, he stood back, took a good look and said "Take that man's name, Corporal, dirty PT vest".

Well it wasn't exactly dirty, just a greyish colour compared with the vests alongside it because it was soaking wet. Nevertheless I had had my name taken and would now be on a charge.

We were out on the Yorkshire wolds for the rest of the week and it wasn't until we returned to Hornsea on the Friday that I was summoned to the Company office to face the music. Now the Army that I was in did not believe in any old nonsense that you were innocent until proved guilty. The fact that you were charged with an offence meant that you must have done something wrong, so it was just a matter of turning up at the office to find out the punishment.

You stood there with your cap in your hand in front of a desk, behind which would be an officer whom you might have vaguely seen in the distance once or twice. The corporal reading out the charge stood alongside you, and standing stiffly to attention behind you would be the Company Sergeant-Major, who would punch you in the back and snarl "Shut up" in your ear if you dared to open your mouth in your defence after the charge was read out.

I went through the whole procedure without saying a word and ended up with five days "confined to barracks". This meant that I had to report to the Company office at every break period and be available for fatigues, but I smiled to myself because for most of the time we were out on exercise where the "jankers" could not apply, or so I thought.

Before I left the sergeant-major told me to report to him on the next day, Saturday, immediately after the midday meal. So while everyone else dressed up and went off to places like Hull to watch rugby league, or to the pictures, I put on my denim fatigue suit and reported to the office. The sergeant-major was waiting for me. He told me to get a bucket, a scrubbing brush and a cloth and to clean all the office floors. This consisted of the ground floor of a house in the better part of town than where we had our billets. He warned me not to rush it in the hope of getting away early because he would be back much later to release me from my task. It was early evening before he returned, had a look at my handiwork and told me to go. He then shook me by ordering me to report to him at the same time the following Saturday.

I went back to the empty billets, not a soul in sight. It was too late to go anywhere or do anything so I went to bed, musing on the injustice that the following Saturday I would again be scrubbing away in solitary splendour and wondering what would happen the Saturday after that. I should have known, because for five consecutive Saturday afternoons I scrubbed out that company office.

The British prisoners were mainly individuals from different regiments, but there were some blocks of men who had suffered a traumatic experience as a complete group, being trapped or ambushed, outnumbered and outgunned.

One such happening had occurred at Villers Bocage, a small village out in front of the British lines. A column of tanks and motorised infantry had made a foray into enemy territory only to be ambushed by a force of Tiger tanks with their huge 88 mm artillery pieces. The column had been shot to pieces until all their hardware was just scrap iron. Those who escaped the carnage were rounded up by the Germans and now found themselves at Alençon. They were men who had fought in North Africa, veterans of desert warfare, men from an elite tank regiment and light infantry battalion, who found it very hard to come to terms with what had happened to them. There were quite a few from the two regiments, all ready to talk about their shattering experience as we were to talk about ours. The words Villers Bocage almost became part of the language as one after another bent our ears, almost with disbelief that such a thing could have happened to them.

We were in a hut occupied mainly by Americans. We spent the days lying on straw palliasses set in two-tier bunks which had been newly made from very raw timber, telling and retelling each other the events which had led up to our capture. One of the Americans was a "Ranger", much older than the rest of us, who had actually scaled cliffs and used explosives at the invasion beaches. He was a quiet sort of person who fatalistically expected a rough time in German hands in the future, something which we didn't even think about. In the next bunk to him was a very young American infantryman, captured at St. Lô, who was a much brasher person. He told me that he came from the "Loop", assuming that everyone knew where the "Loop" was. Much later I discovered that it was part of Chicago. I asked him where he had been stationed in England. He gave this some thought and said that he thought the place was called Llanwern. I told him that it was a village a few miles from Newport, my home town. He told me that he had only been in England for six weeks before the invasion and had never set foot outside the camp. It was as if he had left his home country, travelled thousands of miles and been taken prisoner without any interval.

In the camp there was water available from a tap, so every day I washed out my bandage and had it put back on my arm. The wound healed quickly but still felt very tender to the touch and I couldn't grip anything with my left hand. Once a day, about noon, we lined up for a bowl of watery soup and a piece of black bread. The first time this happened I had great difficulty in stomaching the peculiar bread but having gone so long without food I could not do anything else but eat it. As the days went by I began to accept it as normal.

The camp was just a sloping grassy field with a couple of hangar-like buildings in the middle, a few trestle tables at the top of the slope, from where the soup and bread were dished out, all enclosed by a thick barbed-wire fence. Over to one side, well away from the sheds, tucked up against the fence, was a tent. It appeared that this was where officers taken prisoner were living, not that they deigned to approach us.

I was sitting outside the shed on the thick grass when out of the tent came the Canadian lieutenant, our ex-platoon commander, whom I had last seen in the ditch before I had gone to the farmhouse. He had also been taken and now looked very embarrassed as he approached and offered me a cigarette. Officers obviously had an issue. I accepted the smoke gratefully but didn't have much to say to him, partly because of the natural suspicion of rank carried by most infantrymen. I had always kept away from officers, if only because of the servility they expected, particularly back in England. Not that I had seen much of the platoon commander anyway, because for most of the time we had been led by a sergeant. Occasionally a newly-commissioned officer would be in charge, just to get experience it seemed. I had lost most of my respect for the officer class when, on arrival in Normandy, the first thing they did was to remove the insignia from their uniforms and take up carrying a rifle, to make it difficult to distinguish them from the rest of the soldiery. This was to confuse German snipers who were reportedly picking off officers when they could identify them. I suppose it was just commonsense but it did not make you feel that you were being led by brave warriors.

I couldn't find much to say to the Canadian because I hardly knew him. He had only joined the battalion when we were billeted in barracks in Aldershot, our last station before Normandy. The infantry side of the British army must have been short of line officers. We only had a sergeant for a long time, and just before the invasion quite a few Canadian lieutenants had been drafted into the battalion. This was a bit late in the day to gain the confidence of the men they were supposed to lead. So, looking as demoralised as the rest of us, he wandered back across the field to the tent and I never saw him again.

Chapter four

One day about twenty of us were herded together and put on a heavily guarded lorry which carried us to a small railway station with other buildings around it. One of these was an engine shed in which were two locomotives, full of holes from aircraft cannon shells. None of the buildings had any windows left intact and the walls were heavily scarred from enemy action. It looked as if there had been more than one visitation from enemy aircraft. The railway track itself was showing signs of action, which was the reason we had been brought there. We were each given a long handled shovel and told to start work putting the ballast back between the lines. I was put to work in a narrow cutting with a German guard at each end. On one side were the back gardens of tall French houses. I couldn't do much work with only one good arm, and the able-bodied compatriots with me didn't accomplish much either, but just pretended to scratch away at the small stones. My wounded arm was not a pleasant sight by now, as the blackened blood under the skin had begun to turn a strange yellow colour.

Late in the afternoon there was a scare as a low-flying aircraft shot over the top of us. When it banked for another pass everyone bolted for cover, guards and prisoners alike. I scrambled up the steep side of the cutting and threw myself into the garden of one of the houses as the aircraft flew low over the cutting and then continued on its way.

All was peace and quiet as I turned over and lay on my back to find myself lying among a row of redcurrant bushes. There, silhouetted against a clear blue sky, were lovely long bunches of glistening red fruit. I started to stuff them into my mouth as fast as I could. They tasted like nothing else I had ever eaten, and it brought home to me the fact that I was beginning to feel the effects of not being properly fed.

I was working my way along the row, stripping one bush then sliding on my back to the next, quietly savouring each mouthful, until

I became aware that the German guards were shouting and screaming as they tried to gather up their scattered work gang. I lay still, wondering when they would appear at the top of the cutting, but nobody came so I carried on, lying on my back, working my way through every redcurrant I could find.

Slowly the afternoon wore on and the evening shadows began to fall. I could still hear the guards shouting, so obviously I wasn't the only one still missing. I should have escaped there and then, and I did give it some thought, but all I can say is that I wasn't myself. Maybe if I had had a companion with me I would have had a go, but I didn't, and when I had finished eating all the fruit I quietly slid down the bank to rejoin my fellow prisoners I felt somewhat ashamed of myself, but lying alone in a strange French garden, with one arm useless, not having the slightest idea where I was, and still feeling bemused at being captured, must be my excuses.

The guards were still rushing around, counting heads at the same time, and when they were satisfied that all their charges were present we were hustled away from the railway line and into the lorry for our return journey to the camp. We were not taken out to do work again and after a few days there was a mass evacuation of the camp.

This time the journey was by night, because Allied aircraft were overhead all the time during the day. Even at night, it could be dangerous – at one stage on our journey the convoy was attacked by a plane which dropped flares, lighting up the road. We were driven into the shelter of roadside trees to escape its attentions.

We arrived at what had been a French army barracks in Chartres, where we were locked up with a hundred or so other prisoners in a huge stone floored building with low stone walls dividing the floor into sections, something on the lines of a cattle market.

Once a day we were given a bowl of watery spinach-like soup which held absolutely no nourishment. It was here for the first time that I entered into the bread lottery. As well as the soup, we were issued with a daily bread ration. This consisted of a black, usually mouldy loaf, about the size of a small white loaf, which had to be shared between five prisoners. I got myself organized into a five-man group and we would line up together to get our bread. Watching the loaf carrier very carefully we would return to our niche against one of the low walls.

One of us would then lay the loaf on a bit of rag, and then with a borrowed knife with half a blade, he would attempt to the best of his ability to cut it into five equal pieces. The loaves were misshapen, particularly at the ends, which was generally where most of the mould was, and it was practically impossible to cut five equally good pieces. This caused occasional fights to break out when individuals found that they were being fleeced by the other four. We were all very, very hungry by now and the sight of someone having a small amount of bread extra could only be eased by ensuring that one belonged to a group which could be trusted, and that a proper system was maintained for doling out the pieces of bread.

To overcome this problem, the five pieces of bread were numbered one to five. Five numbered pieces of paper were then put into a steel helmet from which we each drew a number and then claimed the relative piece. Even this system was open to abuse by the unscrupulous so everyone watched every move closely. The crumbs that fell on the piece of rag were allocated daily, in strict rotation, to one of the group. This system, or one like it, prevailed throughout my captivity, whenever we were in a "five men one loaf" situation.

There were also a number of different ways of eating the bread ration, which was about the thickness of two slices of bread. One method was to break it into three pieces and have one at times approximating to normal meal times. Another was to break it in half and have a piece in the morning and a piece before going to sleep. The third way was to eat it all as soon as it was issued. This is what I always did. At least for a fleeting moment I felt something in my stomach and also there was no chance of it being stolen.

We were not confined to the inside of the building but could go outside into a large hard-surfaced area. This was bounded by masses of barbed wire, not a fence but roll after roll of the stuff, something like a World War One defensive position. I used not to go outside with anyone else but would sit on my own with my back against a wooden post, brooding and watching the other prisoners as they mooched about. There weren't very many of us considering the size of the armies which invaded Normandy and the fierce battles which had taken place.

There were some very unusual sights. One prisoner was a Free

French sailor, a matelot, resplendent in his immaculate uniform with polished civilian shoes and French sailor's hat with its red pompom on top. He looked as if he had just arived in port and was heading for a night on the town. He was the only naval person among us. It made me blink my eyes to make sure that the vision was real, and I couldn't for the life of me understand how he had been taken prisoner. There were also two Commandos who stuck tightly together. Both of these were well-dressed, wearing their green berets with cap badges still intact and shining. The unusual prisoners stuck out like a sore thumb compared with the rest of us who looked as if we had slept in our clothes, often bloodstained, as indeed we had for some time even before having been taken prisoner. It was strange to see normal headgear – most of us had nothing or were carrying our steel helmets which the Germans had allowed us to keep.

It was difficult to make out what the buildings had been used for before our arrival. They had obviously been hurriedly converted. The brand new condition of the barbed wire looked as if it had been hastily put into place but the tarmac surface of the outside was very much like a barrack square, and as I sat there brooding it brought back memories of the drill square at the barracks in Aldershot.

As the invasion date drew nearer we had moved down to the South of England from Yorkshire. This was the nearest we had been to home for some time and in reply to a letter of mine, my girlfriend suggested that she came to Aldershot by train for the Whitsun weekend. Preparations for the invasion were speeding up, restrictions were being tightened, and it looked as if something would happen very soon. Despite all this uncertainty I agreed to my girlfriend's suggestion and she wrote to tell me when she would be arriving.

In the week before Whitsun all the battalion transport was loaded up, lashed down, waterproofed and lined up on the barrack square behind the block in which we were billeted. Then what I had feared happened. The battalion was confined to barracks just before the weekend. This meant that I didn't have time to stop my girlfriend making the journey. I just kept my fingers crossed that I could find a solution to the problem.

The Saturday arrived and I was stuck indoors. My girlfriend was due to arrive in the early afternoon, and as the time of her arrival came and went I decided to take a chance. After looking out of the windows and finding that the barrack square was deserted, I changed into my "walking-out" dress and made my way down the back stairs. The barracks consisted of two blocks of balconied buildings facing one another across a narrow road which led to one of the main streets of the town. At this junction was a guard post. The rear of our block led onto the drill square which was covered with waiting transport. Once across the square there was no barrier to the outside world.

Using the trucks as cover I made my way out into the town and along to the railway station. This meant going through busy streets with every possibility of meeting senior NCOs and officers from the battalion. They would be bound to recognise me, even if they didn't know me, because of my cap badge and regimental shoulder flashes, so it was a rather furtive journey. I finally made it to the station, hours late, to find my girl waiting. Although I explained my predicament and the chance I was taking in being out and about at all, I still got a very frosty reception. It appeared that it had not been a very lonely wait because Aldershot at that time was mainly occupied by the Canadian army, and she had not been short of company. I didn't like the idea of moving about the town but the next move was to find somewhere for her to spend the night. I was supposed to have booked a room for her in advance, but being confined to barracks hadn't been able to do so, and this again didn't help matters. It being Whitsun weekend, Aldershot was full of forces' relations and it was very difficult to get in anywhere. We trudged from guest house to guest house, finding them all full, and charging very high prices. I kept looking over my shoulder to make sure that I wasn't spotted by someone in authority.

Eventually we passed a pub with seats outside. The doors opened and we sat down for a refreshing beer. My girl asked the landlord if he knew of anywhere she could be put up for the night. He took pity on her and said that she could stay in the pub provided that she looked after herself. So that was one problem settled, and it soon became dark enough for me to become indistinguishable from any other uniformed individual, so we could move about freely.

I didn't want to be too late going back into the barracks so I dropped my girl off fairly early at the pub. I made my way across town, around to the side of the barracks, slipped through the trucks on the barrack square and got back into the room occupied by my platoon. There I found a great air of excitement. It appeared that there had been an outbreak of indiscipline in my absence, no doubt brought on by the fact that the battalion was confined to barracks. These barracks must have been built at least a hundred years ago. They had great thick walls into which the sun's heat had permeated during the previous couple of weeks' hot weather, so that it was almost impossible to sleep at night. The result was that most people were a bit edgy during the hot days, and being confined to barracks meant that there was nowhere to go to get away from the smelly oppressive rooms. There was also an air of apprehension as to what the outcome of the episode would be. Now I hadn't even been on site at the time but if there was any punishment going then I would be one of the victims as well. I couldn't very well go round saying that I had been in town with my girl during the incident. I would probably have been locked up straightaway.

But I was certainly locked up now, as I gazed at the surrounding barbed wire. There was no easy exit through the wire of this barrack square. Watching the two Commandos it seemed to me that they were weighing up the chances of getting out as they strolled around the perimeter of the square. The fact that escaping even entered my mind meant that I must have been recovering from the initial trauma of having been captured. The only bit of equipment I possesed was my clasp knife. This was attached to a lanyard which I had put around my waist so that the end of the rope passed through the large loop and allowed the knife itself to hang down inside my trouser pocket without actually touching the bottom, which must have been the reason my captor missed it when he first searched me. But I couldn't really see what help it might be. The barbed wire looked impenetrable.

After we had been in the prison at Chartres for a few days, the lack of food really made itself felt. Until then our innate reserves had carried us through, but now we began to get really hungry and I started to suffer from blackouts. Weak with hunger, we lay about apathetically on the stone floor for most of the time. If you got to your feet you felt a strange dizziness come over you and you had to hold on to something for quite a long time until you recovered.

After Chartres I never again experienced blackouts although I went for long periods without any food at all. It must have been that, during this period, my body was adjusting itself to a new set of nutritional circumstances.

One thing that we were now missing was a cigarette. Apart from the occasional rollup scrounged off a German guard, no-one had had a proper smoke since they were captured. One day one of our group of five had a brilliant idea which we put into operation after the bread had been doled out. He suggested that we turn the pockets of our battledress tunics inside out and scrape the bottom of them onto our piece of rag, in case any crumbs of tobacco had fallen down from happier days when we had carried packets of twenty in our breast pockets. We accumulated quite a little pile of khaki-wool fluff, with a few grains of tobacco mixed in, and also some small black specks.

One of the group had a small book of the New Testament with very thin pages. We took out one of the fly pages and carefully rolled the tobacco grained fluff into a thin but passable cigarette. One of us scrounged a match from a Free French prisoner who was actually carrying a suitcase stuffed with all sorts of useful things.

Now we were ready, and we sat on our haunches in a small circle. The match was struck, the cigarette lit, and each of us quickly took a drag on our makeshift roll, sucked in the smoke and held it in our lungs in sheer delight. The sensation did not last long because we all began to splutter and choke as our lungs were bombarded with what seemed to be tiny shafts of fire. We were in agony for a full five minutes, our eyes streaming with tears.

Holding an inquest, we checked the contents of our pockets to find that one of us was carrying a small packet of black pepper. Some of this had escaped into his pocket – these were the black grains we had noticed in the fluff. As we had drawn the smoke from our makeshift roll into our lungs, so we had taken in burning specks of pepper. I never again took part in scraping fluff from pockets for a smoke.

Although we suffered from lack of food, there was plenty of water available. Every day I took my bandage off, washed it and had someone put it back on for me. The bullet holes, one at the front of my arm and one at the back, were quite small and healing rapidly, but the arm stayed swollen with congealed blood which was by now a mottled black and yellow.

After about a week at Chartres we were all issued with a card, a pre-printed postcard-sized piece of brown cardboard which we were told to address home to let our relatives know that we had been captured. There were a number of statements on the card and we were told to cross out those statements which did not apply to us. The first statement was that I had been taken prisoner, which was not for crossing out. I felt miserable about letting my friends and family know my plight, but it was better than them not knowing what had happened to me. Another statement was that I had been wounded. This sounded rather vague to me as there were no indications as to how serious the wounds might be. I decided to cross this one out so that those at home would not have any worry about me apart from the fact that I was a prisoner. I then signed my name with my fountain pen which I still had on me and handed the card in. At least, if it got through, my situation would be known.

Towards the end of our stay at Chartres we were joined by a group of prisoners who had been wounded before capture and taken to hospital at Alençon. One of these was from my company. He had received a large piece of shrapnel in his buttock and the last that was seen of him was in a German staff car, well part of him at least, because he had his feet on the floor of the car, hands on the rear seat, with his bandaged bottom sticking up above the side of the open car.

They had been well tended in the French hospital where, although heavily guarded, they were looked after by French orderlies who kept them informed about the progress of the war. As the weeks wore on they learned that the Americans had broken through and were getting progressively nearer to the hospital, so their hopes grew that they might soon be freed. But it was not to be. One day there was a great panic and all the prisoners except the most seriously wounded were moved out in a hurry. All their hopes of freedom vanished and here they were in the bag with the rest of us, having to come to terms with the type of existence which we had been enduring for some time.

Although we felt sorry for their bad luck we welcomed the news that it appeared that the allies were doing well. Until then we had had no idea at all of what was happening in the outside world. Maybe the war wouldn't last long after all and we would soon be home again.

Chapter five

We were in Chartres for a few weeks and then we were herded into single decker buses painted in camouflage colours. They were covered in netting with branches of trees and bushes stuck into the mesh to increase the camouflage further.

We arrived at our destination in the early morning – Paris. The buses stopped outside a park in the suburbs of the city and we were ordered out to line up on the road outside. There the guards made us remove our bootlaces and belts. They then cut off the buttons from our trousers which attached them to our battledress blouses and finally they cut the buttons off our flies. This meant that as we moved off we had to hold up our trousers with our hands and shuffle along as best we could in our laceless boots.

We shuffled some miles through Paris with armed guards on either side of our column, with French civilians trying hard to ignore us as they passed by on the pavements. How different from the time we had marched down the Rhondda valley.

At the end of our recruitment training in Brecon we were different animals from when we arrived months before in our civilian clothing. Our heavy new hobnailed boots had been broken in by a series of route marches, starting with a five mile one, which left our feet blistered and bleeding. We progressed until fifteen miles meant nothing to us, and now to complete our route march training we were to embark on a three-day jaunt, marching during the day and in the evening giving the local Home Guard an insight into the type of general training we had been through.

The first part of our trip was by lorry from Brecon over the Beacons to Hirwaun at the very head of the road which led down into the Rhondda Valley. We got out of the lorries, lined up in sections of nine men, and set off down the road, each section keeping its distance from the next which was on the opposite side, with the one after that back on the same side as ourselves. There were nine sections all told so we were strung out for quite a distance. We looked very professional in that sort of lineup, wearing our steel helmets, webbing equipment and with rifles slung over our shoulders, just to show the Home Guard how it was done, which was a bit of a cheek really when you consider that we had only been in uniform ourselves for a couple of months.

We marched for a few miles along a road that was in quite a bleak area with no houses at all in sight and dull scenery all around. Then suddenly the valley opened up in front of us into a magnificent view that was a pleasure to march into. It was like a huge soup spoon with a large round bowl on the right leading down to the handle which was the valley itself. Steadily down we went around the curve of the bowl, along a narrow road completely free from traffic with no-one else in sight, with the only sound the tramping of our studded boots on the tarmac. It was a beautiful day in midsummer and I felt quite sorry when we finally reached the bottom of the bowl and saw the terraced houses of the Rhondda in front of us. It wasn't long before we found ourselves in the village of Treherbert where we were to spend the night.

We were to sleep in a hall, actually a large wooden shed, on the bare wooden boards which gave me the first taste of the sleeping conditions that I was going to encounter as a footsoldier from then on. But first we had a meal from the lorries which came over from Brecon with food and blankets. Then we fell in to give the Home Guard an exhibition of "battle drill". This was a drill, dreamed up by someone, to be performed on the barrack square, movements that were carried out by shouted orders supposed to simulate an attack on an enemy position by a section, a platoon or a company. It consisted mainly of flanking movements and giving covering fire to other sections or platoons which advanced in stages on the objective. These manoeuvres were accompanied by shouted instructions of "Number one section, left flanking!" at which Number One would march smartly off to the left and take up a position, at attention, on the left of the barrack square, and then other sections would be moved about by shouted orders. I suppose someone was harking back to the days before the machine gun, when foot regiments formed squares and repelled attacks by firing to orders such as "Front rank, fire! Rear rank, fire!". These operations could be well practised and perfected on the barrack square before being put to practical use on the battlefield but even we raw soldiers didn't see much practical application for them in the conditions of the times.

The barrack square at Brecon was huge, and well able to accommodate a company for battle drill, but at the head of the Rhondda there was really no flat space of that size. We had to carry out the exhibition on the side of the mountain, watched by contingents of the Home Guard from the surrounding area. It was the time of year when summer evenings were long and we kept going until dusk finally fell upon the hillside and we were dismissed to return to our hard floor bunks to sleep the night away gratefully.

Early next morning we were up for a quick wash under a cold water tap, folded our blankets and handed them back into the lorry which now doled out breakfast from heat-retaining containers. We generally tidied up and then fell in in the same order as the previous day for the march down the valley. Whereas yesterday's march had been through open countryside, we now found ourselves moving along a narrow road which led down through row after row of terraced houses where front doors opened directly onto narrow pavements. We were going down through Treherbert, Treorchy, Pentre, Rhondda Gelli and towards Porth, but so closely linked were the rows of houses that it was difficult to tell where one village started and another ended.

We marched along quite slowly and as we did so the pavements on both sides filled up with people, mainly women and children, who seemed delighted to see us and as we moved along began to press small gifts into our hands. Many of them may have had husbands or fathers in the forces and it appeared that part of the exercise we were in was to "show the flag" to a part of the country which was in quite an out of the way place. Cigarettes weren't easy to come by in the shops, and we could hardly afford them anyway, so it was with great gratitude that we accepted gifts of packets of five Woodbines in their green wrappers which were shyly given to us as women appeared in their doorways and then dashed back indoors to get something for us. If they didn't have any cigarettes then they gave a shilling or two instead, telling us to buy a packet. Some of them even went running into the corner shop and came out with more than one packet. These people seemed to have an affinity with us and to know that a packet of five Woodbines was worth its weight in gold to us, with the meagre pay we received.

We were moving along at about three miles an hour. At the end of an hour's marching a whistle would blow, we would halt and fall out for a ten minute break. It was quite warm weather, so we would lie on our backs on the pavement with our boots in the air, resting on the windowsills of the terraced houses, which seemed to cool our feet off. This break in the marching gave the women from the houses an opportunity to come out with jugs of tea and home made cake. This completely spoilt us for our midday meal of haversack rations which usually consisted of dried up cheese sandwiches. Some lucky ones were actually invited into houses for a sitdown cup of tea and food. When the whistle went after ten minutes, there was great difficulty in winkling them out again to get the show on the road, with our training sergeants racing up and down the road yelling their heads off and blowing their whistles like mad. All this, and our slow movement, meant that it was late in the evening before we reached our destination way down the valley for another night on the bare boards of a wooden hut.

We were told that the next morning we were going to make a mock attack on the Home Guard at Miskin, a village below Mountain Ash. This was on the other side of the mountain in a valley parallel to ours. We were issued with blank ammunition and thunderflashes and told to get some sleep after we had had our evening meal from the lorries again, because we would be up at a very early hour to make a surprise attack. So we were, and with the light just in the sky we began trudging up a narrow road across the mountain on the way to Ynys-y-Bwl, a village at the top of the mountain. But before we reached there, we left the road and took to the rough mountain itself. Somebody had worked out that the Home Guard at Miskin would probably have scouts out on the roads into the village who would send a warning back. Hopefully by making our way across open country we could avoid detection. Soon we were over the top and making our way down the steep mountainside with its tussocks of yellow long ripe grass. Quietly we went along until we reached the back garden walls of the single row of terraced houses which lined the main street of the village, the same as those in the valley which we had just left. Still very early in the morning, we crouched behind the walls undetected and then we were over the top, up the gardens, opening the back doors. People didn't lock their back doors, and we rushed down the passageways with a great hammering of boots to the front doors, opening them up to find ourselves on the main road, firing blank ammunition, throwing thunderflashes and generally making a great deal of noise. There was little evidence of the Miskin Home Guard and it appeared that they were in defensive positions outside the village. Nobody seemed to mind the commotion at such an early hour, nor that we had rushed uninvited through their homes. It seemed that it had all been a great success and a help to the war effort, and we were waved off as the lorries carried us back up the valley and over the Beacons to Brecon.

On a different march this time, we finally arrived at the Gare de L'Ouest. Outside this railway station there was a large cobbled square and here we were made to sit down while the guards encircled us. One station building was occupied by the German army with uniformed German women working there, looking out of the windows at us and coming and going from the building into the station proper, passing quite close to us. This became embarrassing because we were held all day, until darkness fell, in the same spot, and to relieve oneself one had to perform in full view of the German women.

As darkness deepened we were lined up and led into the station to a train of cattle wagons with barbed wire covering all the openings. We were divided into groups of forty, given a large, already opened tin of meat between two and a loaf of black bread each, and then each forty were pushed into a cattle truck. The sliding doors were slammed into position and we were left to sort ourselves out.

I found myself in a wagon with thirty-odd Free French soldiers, most of whom could not speak English, and paired up with a paratrooper wearing the shoulder tabs of Fiji on his battledress.

We stood looking out of the barbed wire covered openings at the lights and movement of the Germans in the station until the train began to move out into the blackness of the countryside. At first we sat down with our backs against the walls of the truck, and then as the night wore on we stretched out to sleep on the wooden floor. Travelling in cattle wagons took on a definite pattern at night. We slept twenty to each side like sardines in a can, and were so tightly packed that when one turned in his sleep, we all turned.

The train moved along through the night with numerous stops and starts. When we stopped we could hear the guards taking up position outside with much shouting and banging. When the train restarted we were thrown about on the hard floor. So, all in all, we did not get a lot of sleep, and the next day was much the same with the train not appearing to make much headway.

Chugging very slowly along, we stood and gazed through the open barbed wire covered holes in the side of the truck. At one point we moved through a small country railway halt. No buildings, just small platforms set in a sort of cutting, completely deserted, except on one platform stood an immaculately dressed, jackbooted German officer, completely alone as if waiting for a train, not that there were many of those about. As we moved very slowly past him, whistles, jeers and catcalls came from every truck. We had picked up a few words of German and shouts of "Deutschland Kaput!" were let loose, this as a result of the information of the Allied breakthrough given to us by our wounded friends, which had raised our morale considerably.

It was funny that although we were on the whole quite fearful of what the Germans might do to us, because we were in a moving train and the object of our vituperation was on a station platform, we felt quite safe in letting him feel the full blast of our abuse. If nothing else, it gave us some satisfaction and release from the pent-up emotions that had been generated from the moment we were captured, not that it had the slightest effect on the German as far as we could tell, although I suppose we hoped that shouts of "Deutschland Kaput" might dent his morale a little. Nobody enjoyed being a prisoner of war, particularly being captured when in an attacking army, and anything to show that we were still anti-German was helpful.

That morning I offered half of the tin of meat to my Fijian companion, but he shook his head, so I ate the lot. On looking at him, he appeared to be completely shattered. I felt lost myself, but he from as far away as Fiji must have been completely demoralised and he looked it.

We had no idea how long we would be on the train, but obviously it was going to be a long journey because we had been issued with so much food. I carefully cut a piece of bread and ate it with the meat, and then pushed the balance of the loaf into my shirt beneath the battledress.

I was now beginning to feel the cold in my arm at nights, so although my wound had healed I kept the bandage on as a sort of sleeve which gave me some warmth at least where I was injured. Time and again I wished that my shirt and battledress sleeves had been slit up from the wrist rather than hacked off from above the elbow, as I tried to tuck my arm into my battledress blouse in an effort to keep warm in the middle of the dark nights in the cold and draughty cattle truck.

At the station in Paris I had been separated from the group that I usually spent my time with, which was a lesson in itself, and got pushed into a truck with people I had hardly seen before, most of whom were French speaking. My friend George and I, being of roughly the same age and background, were good company for each other, and now here I was with no-one to talk to. The Fijian could hardly speak English and just grunted occasionally. On the other side of me was the rear wall of the truck, because I had opted for the corner as looking like a more comfortable position. So there I sat, day after day, with nothing better to do than think about old times. Being constantly aware that I was in a train, there being no form of springing it seemed, took my thoughts to my last train journey.

That was when we left Aldershot for the coast. We had been trucked to the military railway station, which we didn't even know existed, and the seven of us from our section took over one compartment. There was one platform, with a single line, and on the other side was a long low line of offices. Through the windows of these we could see a large number of girls working away. As the train pulled out we jammed the window open to wave our farewells. The girls came to the windows to wave us off and we could see that most of them were in tears. We didn't take a lot of notice, thinking that they were sorry that we were leaving the area, but they must have had more understanding of what we were heading for than they did, because by the time I was captured, only two of the seven were still in the land of the living.

I wasn't in a pleasant frame of mind at the best of times in that cattle truck, and the thought of my fallen comrades made me deliberately turn my thoughts to the train trip before last.

The last home leave before the invasion had been taken by the whole company. A special train was laid on to carry us back to Yorkshire from South Wales. I was supposed to catch it at Newport but it had started at the heads of the valleys and was full by the time it arrived. My girl had come to see me off and I stood out like a sore thumb, there being only a few soldiers on the platform. The windows of the carriages were full of men from Nantyglo and Blaina, Ebbw Vale, Tredegar and the other valley coal and steel towns. Men with names like Jones (lots of them), Belli and Zobole from the well-established Italian communities, all whistling and catcalling as I kissed my girl goodbye and clambered aboard. Where were they now, mostly dead in one short summer's afternoon. I couldn't escape from these morbid thoughts no matter how I tried.

From this "embarkation" leave, one of our number was unfortunately late arriving back in his billet at Hornsea. We were supposed to be back by midnight on a given date but he missed his train and did not arrive back until after reveille the next day. A zealous NCO, and there were plenty of those, reported him absent, and when he saw him arrive, charged him with being absent without leave. The charge was dealt with very quickly. He was sentenced to twenty-eight days in a military prison. This information was well-publicised by the authorities, to let us know that things were becoming serious and to act as a deterrent.

A corporal and a private escorted him to the military prison by train. They came back visibly shaken and told us that all three of them were treated as prisoners as soon as the gates opened in front of them. They had to run on the spot and wherever they went were made to move at the double, and were all abused verbally. The two escorts were very glad when the gates closed behind them on their way out.

On his return from jail the prisoner told us of his experiences, which had turned him into a very serious and obedient soldier. He had had a very miserable month to say the least. It started with having to move about on the double wherever he went, and being continually abused. Each morning his kit had to be laid out in a certain order on his bed, ready for inspection. For quite a while, each morning at the inspection his kit was torn apart and he had to do it again. Eventually he got it right and then rather than break it up to sleep on the bed he left it intact and slept on the floor. Not that he got much sleep. Every night a rusty piece of metal was handed to him, for example an old stirrup. This had to be cleaned and polished, using a piece of rag and the sand from a fire bucket in his cell, and then handed in by the morning in pristine condition to avoid further punishment.

The days were spent moving a pile of coal from one corner of the exercise yard to another freshly whitewashed corner, all at the double. The corner had to be spotlessly clean, with every speck of coal dust removed, before it was whitewashed ready for the next day's exercise when it was moved back again.

For the midday meal he was given only one container, so that potatoes, meat and gravy were topped up with the pudding which invariably had custard with it. He could put up with all the rest, but this had made him feel like a trapped animal. The treatment had definitely made a good soldier of him, but it disgusted us that someone as well-behaved as he, who had never been in trouble before, had been made a scapegoat supposedly to deter the rest of us. Why we were supposed to need a deterrent I don't know – no-one I knew had ever let the thought of absconding enter their heads, and if there were the odd bad egg then the thought of punishment would make no difference to their actions.

We were in the truck for four or five days. Progress was very slow and during the day we would stand and look longingly out of the openings at the French countryside. At one period the train ran alongside a river, a green languid French river with anglers fishing on its banks. The sight of this made me realise how much of a prisoner I was, with the outside world totally cut off.

There were no toilet facilities in the truck. To pass water we had a tin into which we relieved ourselves and then threw it out of the openings. When we opened our bowels we did it on a piece of paper and then threw it outside. All this in full view of thirty-nine pairs of strange eyes which had nothing better to do than just sit there and watch.

What we could do nothing about was thirst. We had no water and no hope of getting any, and so just had to suffer it out.

At last the train came to a halt, the doors opened and we were ordered out to find ourselves on a station platform outside a barracks at Châlons-sur-Marne.

The guards here had a carefree, arrogant air now that we were so far from the fighting. Obviously they did not appreciate the situation in Normandy. We were lined up and moved slowly along to the barbed wire gates in single file. A lot of us were still wearing our steel helmets. The Americans had their webbing belts with water bottles attached to them. As we neared the gates, so the guards told us to throw our helmets and other equipment onto a heap. This was accompanied by much ribaldry, aimed mainly at the Americans whose belongings were described as coming from Woolworths, all this in strong American-accented English from the German guards.

The barracks into which we were pushed had once been a French cavalry barracks for colonial troops, and some of these, probably Moroccans, could be glimpsed from time to time.

We found ourselves in a most peculiar situation. Prisoners from the Second Front were housed in two small separate blocks of several-storied buildings. The block which we found ourselves in was jammed to bursting point with only a small outside area for fresh air, and bare boards to sleep on in the rooms inside. The food situation was virtually nil with only the five men to a loaf ration each day.

The block across the way was empty and we were told that it contained Red Cross parcels. These, which we had never seen, held out visions of delight. But it appeared that the only way in which one could be transferred to this paradise was to offer to be interrogated and volunteer information to the enemy. Nobody would do so and the two blocks remained separated by a wide gulf.

We were in Châlons for about a week, getting steadily hungrier and then suddenly we were moved en bloc across to the other block and told to stand around. Whether this was because our original block was becoming overcrowded or whether the fighting had suddenly got nearer was the subject of much discussion.

After some hours of waiting around we were lined up, passed out through a door and issued with a loaf of bread each and a British Red Cross parcel between two. We then moved on outside the prison to another waiting cattle truck where forty of us were herded into each truck again. We settled down against the walls of the truck and feverishly opened the parcels to see what they contained. The tinned food had been opened, presumably to prevent food hoarding which might help with escapes.

Starving, George and I ate through a lot of our parcel. It was good to have the two of us together sharing the food. We trusted one another and could be quite amicable about which of the delicacies to start on, whereas with a stranger it could be quite difficult, particularly when one was ravenously hungry. Also, it was good to have someone to talk to for the journey ahead. We had learned our lesson in Paris and had stood tightly together as we were bundled into forties, inveigling ourselves into the middle of a bunch.

It was our first experience of Red Cross parcels and a marvellous one at that. The one we had between us was a British parcel. This was a cardboard box about the size of a shoe box, packed so that there was not an inch of room left. British Red Cross parcels contained no frills but were obviously designed to give the maximum nourishment. This they did in no small way - someone must have known that prisoners of the Germans were very poorly fed and had planned the parcels accordingly. It was a good thing that they had done so, because although we only had the occasional parcel, or more usually part of one, it always seemed to arrive when we were at a particularly low ebb and beginning to feel weak from lack of nourishment, and would pull us round. There's no doubt that without the Red Cross parcels I would not have survived.

Chapter six

The cattle wagon had a milk churn in the middle of the floor which held drinking water, and now that we had empty tins from the Red Cross parcels, we were able to drink from it. We were in the train for five days before the doors opened again. We stopped, started, shunted backwards and forwards, sometimes waiting for half a day in some siding or other. It was now well into summer and the weather was very hot. The water in the churn soon ran out with forty thirsty men helping themselves from it.

Relieving oneself again became a problem so as not to despoil our cramped quarters. With receptacles now in abundance we were able to pass water into a tin and then throw it out of the openings, and with Red Cross parcel cardboard boxes we could tear off a piece, empty our bowels onto it and throw it out onto the track. One corner of the truck was allocated for this in the daytime but at night it was impossible with twenty men a side lying down and occupying the whole area.

After a day the milk churn was empty. Someone had a bright idea. Why not use the churn as a toilet? The top of the churn was about six inches in diameter and this made it a difficult operation. The churn was positioned near the end wall of the truck and it was a peculiar predicament to find oneself perched on top of a swaying six inch hole as the train clanged and banged its way along, straining to empty one's bowels with a tin held in front to pass water into. All this with thirty-nine pairs of eyes with nothing better to do than watch you perform. With forty men using the churn it soon filled and then became a source of embarrassment. It was so full that as the train swayed and clanked along, excrement slopped over the top. One end of the truck became uninhabitable, and we were more and more jammed up at the other end. We were unable to stretch out to sleep at night and had to take turns sitting with our knees up.

As the days wore on, thirst again became a problem, whereas we were still relatively well off for food. We had bits of our Red Cross parcels left and chunks of bread which were jealously guarded day and night. I always kept my bread tucked in my shirt and my parcel bits and pieces in various pockets. We had become suspicious of everybody when it came to food of any description.

After five days the train pulled into a station, the doors slid back and we were allowed out onto the platform one truck at a time, dirty, unshaven and smelling. A few of us were allowed to pull the churn out and we then emptied it into a lavatory with much shaking and swilling around of its contents. We then took it to what looked like a fire hydrant. When the valve was opened water gushed out in a great stream. Taking advantage of this flow I put my head under it. It felt marvellous but I soon got a clout from a guard's gun butt which moved me away. We then washed out the churn, filled it up with water and hauled it back into the truck so that everyone on board could have a drink. It appeared that we were in Metz, wherever that was, but by the sound of it either Germany or very near.

The doors of the truck stayed open with two armed guards occupying the entrance. As the train finally pulled out of the station they stayed that way with the guards laughing and gesticulating as we began to run through the German countryside. This did not last for long, and when the train made one of its usual innumerable stops the doors were slammed shut again. We spent another night in the train and then we pulled into a siding at a place we were told was called Limburg, in heavily wooded countryside.

After some time we were shouted out of our trucks, lined up and marched into a large prisoner of war camp. As we made our way along a barbed-wire fenced roadway we passed a line of long low huts. Peering through the windows we could see the faces of Indian prisoners who waved to us. Probably captured in the Western Desert, we thought, as we made our way to the camp's football pitch.

We sat around for hours until we were ordered to our feet and lined up in threes to be counted for the first time. Germans must be the worst counters of people in the world. No two of them could arrive at the same number and we were counted over and over again, a situation which was to become familiar to us.

A German officer then addressed us in very good English. He told us that as invaders of Europe we were considered to be gangsters and that as such we were not going to be treated as were the other prisoners in the camp. With that we were marched off to a large building where we were to have a hot shower.

The building had quite a low ceiling with a large number of shower outlets set into it. When we stripped off and stood underneath we looked up rather apprehensively. We had all heard how the Jews had been taken into such rooms, and instead of water coming out of the sprays, cyanide gas had engulfed and destroyed them.

But hot water came out of the nozzles and for the first time in months I felt clean. We dried ourselves on our shirts, got dressed and were marched along to a large wired compound in which there were a number of very large tents, marquees almost as big as circus tents. The floors were covered to a depth of three feet or more with what can be described as clean litter I suppose, a sort of papery wooden substance which was quite soft to lie on.

The compound also had a latrine, alongside which were a series of taps on a piece of board, which looked as if it had been put up in a hurry. After our experiences until then the place was relatively civilised, and we joined a large crowd of prisoners of all nationalities.

By now summer was well advanced and day after day the hot sun shone down. We were back on a fifth of a loaf a day. Once a day large containers of watery soup were hauled into the compound. We lined up for this, and the soup was doled out into the tin cans we had saved from the Red Cross parcels. I still adopted the attitude of eating my bread all at one go, but those of us who kept a piece for the morning ran into all sorts of hazards.

The daylight hours were spent stripped to our underpants sitting in the hot sun. At night we retreated into the large tents to sleep. Bread savers would often put their bread into a piece of rag, make a small hole in the litter and then lie down to sleep on top of it. But there were sharp eyes about. As the night wore on, tunnelling operations would begin as bread thieves wormed their way underneath the sleepers to get at their food. Almost invariably they would wake the proposed victim. Uproar and savage fights would break out at odd intervals through the night. With my system of eating the bread at one go, at least for an hour or so one felt less hungry and could sleep soundly.

The compound we were in was in the middle of the camp. At night it was pitch dark with not a glimmer of light to be seen anywhere, and was surrounded by a thick barrier of barbed wire except for the entrance which consisted of a pair of large wooden gates covered in a lattice of barbed wire which left openings of about a foot square. In the middle of the night, when it was at its darkest, the shadowy figure of a German sentry would appear at the gate to barter bread for gold.

This apparition began to appear after we had been in the camp for some time. His timing was right, because by then with only a loaf to five men a day we were beginning to get weak with hunger and would do anything for bread. The German was after gold watches and rings, particularly the latter, of which there were quite a few on the fingers of Allied prisoners which were exchanged for a loaf. Hopefully one night I approached the group at the gates, holding out my fountain pen with its gold nib, a present from my girlfriend. When I held the pen through the wire the German brusquely pushed it aside. He was after much more profitable business. So I went back into the tent and lay down as hungry as ever, thinking that there must be plenty of food about somewhere. I wondered what sort of food German prisoners in England were having and thought that the British surely wouldn't treat their captives as the Germans did.

I hadn't come across any German prisoners at home but I had seen Italians riding around in lorries in the English countryside on their way to and from work on farms, most of them big strapping fellows who looked well fed. It could well be the German mentality which was denying us sustenance. I wondered what the Americans alongside us were thinking, because I would have bet my bottom dollar that German prisoners who had been transported to America and Canada were not going hungry, and certainly not undergoing the five men to a loaf regime.

One day the Indian prisoners, obviously realising the plight we were in, made us a present of some of their food. When the large containers, in which the watery soup normally came, arrived, they were full of cooked rice with sultanas and raisins. We were also given a chapati each as we lined up with our rusty tins.

On a diet of watery soup and a fifth of a loaf a day there was no doubt that we would eventually die of starvation. The Indians' gift helped us to survive those first few weeks as we sat around apathetically.

I used to lie down on the paper-like surface of the large tent and think about food. I remembered the recruiting centre at Brecon where the myths about army food had tended to curtail my appetite when I first arrived there. Even at the end of my training I still hadn't got used to the food. This all changed when I was posted to a battalion stationed just outside Cambridge. The camp consisted of large tents set on the side of a sloping field surrounded by thick woods. This was probably quite pleasant in summer but winter was upon us with its short hours of daylight. The weather was very unkind with continual rain and low mist which hung about eerily in the woods.

Our tent was at the top of the slope. The floor was covered in tarpaulins and a deep trench had been dug all round to divert rain water away. The dining tent was below us and had no protective trench. Breakfast was served very early in the morning and at that time of the year we had to make our way from sleeping quarters to the mess tent in pitch darkness, usually in heavy rain, with two mess tins in our mittened hands. Not having a mug for tea meant that to get the full amount of food on offer one had to use a certain amount of ingenuity plus dexterity. The menu consisted of three items: a drink of tea, porridge, a meat dish for example liver or sausages, always accompanied by mashed potatoes and a thick slice of bread from a cottage loaf.

On arrival at the mess tent, where one would be partially blinded by the light from a couple of paraffin pressure lanterns hanging over the trestle tables at the entrance where the food waited to be served, one would hold two mess tins in the left hand with the collapsible handles crossed for stability. With the right hand, one would pick up a thick slice of bread, manoeuvring it flat onto the palm of the hand, and then make one's way along the line. The first mess tin would be held out for a dollop of thick porridge. The bread would be held out for a large portion of mashed potato, followed by the ration of liver and gravy. The empty mess tin would then be filled with hot tea, and this needed some dexterity while keeping an eye on the bread, mashed potato and liver. It was very tricky making one's way into the half darkness of the tent with the only light coming from the lamps at the entrance, across a muddy floor to the rickety benches and tables. The ground underfoot was of a red soil and as one sat there eating breakfast the heavy rain outside would send rivulets of red mud around the feet. The first meal I had in these conditions came as something of a shock after the mess hall in Brecon with its proper building, thick white plates and pint china mugs and food served from stainless steel counter tops in a very clean and hygienic atmosphere. By comparison with the food at Cambridge, it was a gourmet's delight.

I wasn't with the battalion for very long before I was made a lance-corporal and sent back to Brecon for an NCO's course. Part of my duties were to sit with recruits in the dining hall and supervise their meals. I thought I was in heaven after Cambridge. The main course at the midday meal was picked up on a self-service basis, but the "sweet" was collected along with large, thick white plates of the soup variety and brought to the head of the table where I dished it out to the dozen or so raw recruits. The "sweet" came in a large round tin, about twice the size of a cake tin, which would be threequarters full with such delicacies as milky sweet rice pudding with a beautiful golden skin on the top, enough for twelve large helpings.

Initially recruits would have difficulty in getting used to the army style main course and often would not fancy any second course at all, which meant that sometimes I would sit there at an empty table, after they had all gone, looking down at an untouched large tin of delicious food for my own consumption. Sometimes I felt so bloated that I had difficulty getting up from the table and it was almost impossible to take part successfully in any kind of vigorous exercise in the afternoon.

Eventually the recruits would get used to the food and this, together with all the fresh air and exercise they were getting, meant that they would start to eat the sweet course. But even here I could beat the system by giving out smallish portions to the others and keeping a large remainder for myself, despite some of the accusing glances I was given. It wasn't as satisfactory as keeping the whole tin to myself but it was a lot better than a normal helping.

This time came to an end when at the end of the course I was transferred to the battalion with which I came to Normandy. I could have stayed in Brecon if I had been really serious about training recruits, but my heart wasn't in it. That wasn't why I had joined the army – I might just as well have stayed in my job which was probably of more value to the war effort. I carried this frame of mind with me all the time during my service. I wanted the adventure of being a fighting man living in the fresh air and being fit and strong. I was also very interested in girls, and this combined with my need for adventurous living meant that I didn't take army life seriously enough, with the end result that I left the relative comforts and easy living of the recruiting centre for pastures new.

The thoughts of the "fleshpots" of Brecon made my mouth water. I could even see the golden brown skin on the top of the rice pudding in my daydreams.

Finally the Germans relented and gave out some Red Cross parcels. The first one was shared among five people, and the next between two. We were in the compound for four or five weeks and received several parcels, never more than one between two. This kept us alive if not lively. The tins were always opened or punctured by the Germans so that in the hot weather we had to eat them up as soon as possible.

It was now that looseness of the bowels became a part of life. Whenever one ate anything apart from black bread and watery soup then one soon had to rush to the latrine. Some people were so badly affected that it was not unusual to go to the latrine and find people sitting on the lavatories with their trousers down around their ankles eating their way through a tin of Red Cross salmon.

We were issued either with British or American parcels, presumably because of the mixed nationalities in the compound. Whenever it was rumoured that an issue was to be made, quiet speculation would arise as to which type it would be. The British ones were more practical and better from a nutritional point of view, containing such things as bully beef, salmon and jam. The American ones had things like tins of peanut butter or dried milk called Klim, and even large tablets of a beautiful white soap.

One thing that we did not have was a cup of tea, even with the makings of tea, sugar and dried milk from the parcels, because we had no hot water. It had been a long time since I'd had a decent mug of tea, a large white mug, army pattern, which must have held a good pint, way back in Haywards Heath.

We had arrived by train at Haywards Heath from Aldershot to spend some time under canvas before embarking on infantry carrier lorries for the journey to the coast. Our route took us through several small villages and then through a fairly large town. As we rode down the main street we could see women out shopping with little children at their side. They took not the slightest notice of us – they must have seen tens of thousands of troops making the same journey. Then someone in our truck put his hand in his pocket, pulled out what little money he had, mainly copper coins, and flung it to the children. I suppose he must have reasoned that English money would be no use to him on the other side of the Channel. This made sense to most of us and we all began throwing coins to the children until our pockets were empty. It was a very rare day when we had paper money, so that most of us got out of the lorries at Newhaven without a penny to our names.

We found ourselves in a paved area outside a maze of wire mesh corridors and barbed wire fences obviously protecting the harbour, although why anyone should want to stowaway to Normandy was beyond reason. Sorting ourselves out into sections, piling our heavy load of equipment into a neat stack, we sat down on the ground to await our next move. Waiting around was standard practice for us, as infantrymen we spent most of our time doing just that, but this was different - we were off on the ultimate adventure. Young soldiers like myself were eager to be off and away and into battle. We found all the waiting around difficult. Older soldiers, say in their late twenties, were not so happy, standing around with thoughtful faces and some were even quite irritable with us eager beavers. They had more sense than we did, and probably had responsibilities such as wives and children back home which was something that we younger ones could just not appreciate.

And so we sat around on the hard tarmac, no brass bands playing, no flags waving as we waited to embark for the Channel crossing just like any other time we had hung around waiting for the next move. We were there for hours, and after a while we could have done with a cup of tea. Just at the entrance to the wire fence was a mobile canteen staffed by civilian women from some sort of voluntary organisation. But tea cost a penny a cup and most of us had thrown away our money on the way down, thinking that it would be a long time before we had any need of it.

There were those among us, however, the tight-fisted ones, who had found it impossible to throw their money away. We knew who they were likely to be from living in such close quarters with them. Thinking that it was about time they realised that English money would shortly be of no use to them at all, we tried to persuade them to treat us to a cup of tea. But to no avail, they just refused to change their ways. Because no-one else went to the canteen, the tight-fisted ones also stayed away for fear of being ridiculed. There wasn't much evidence of comradeship – more like every man for himself.

The women running the tea stall must have found it most peculiar that they were surrounded for hours on end by soldiery and yet no-one at all came up to buy anything. When you think about it, there we were, about to go to France to fight for King and Country, you would think that someone might have given us a cup of tea. But it was not to be. The last chance to have a cup of tea had vanished and it looked as if it would be a long time before we managed to brew up.

With the parcels we now had currency, because they contained cigarettes as well as food. British parcels usually had fifty cigarettes, either in a tin or in cellophane packets of ten Players. If they were in a tin you had fifty, if in packets sometimes more. The American parcels could have as many as seven packets of twenty Chesterfield or Camel. So one was never quite sure what one wanted – American parcels were more exciting because of the uncertainty about numbers of cigarettes. Cigarettes were the bargaining counter, although when British parcels were issued, Americans were always around trying to swap things like tins of jam for tins of salmon. With five cigarettes I was able to buy a piece of blanket big enough to wrap around my arm. By tying it around with a piece of string I was able to sleep more comfortably. The days were hot but the nights could go off quite cold, and up until then I had experienced quite a bit of discomfort, so that my piece of blanket was a blessing.

The daily bread ration of five men to a loaf had made me part of a team that stuck together once we trusted each other. Initially one could be a part of any five and this could leave you with the smallest share if the other four were organised against you. So finally we coalesced into groups of five which each had its own ritual. Our five consisted of me, George Pepper, a rifleman from an English infantry battalion whom I had bumped into on and off since Normandy, a dark-haired gunner from a tank destroyed at Villers Bocage, and another member of my own regiment. We were a very diverse group, typical of the mass of prisoners as a whole. Even men from the same outfits tended to split off if they were from a different part of the country from the rest of a group that had been captured. This diversity seemed to make our little group settle down together at any time. Not really knowing anything about each other's private lives, or faults, allowed us to accept the others at face value and only to consider their personalities in the light of their reaction to the unpleasant and unhealthy situation we found ourselves in.

With cigarettes the dark-haired tank gunner had bought a pack of dogeared playing cards from God knows where. Someone else had managed to get hold of a stub of pencil and with plenty of Red Cross cardboard we were all set up to play Gin Rummy.

The weeks we spent in the compound were hot and sunny. We sat in the sun, stripped to the waist, with our bleached hair getting longer and our beards sprouting. We would crawl out of the tents as soon as the day was warm enough, take up a position near the latrines which gave protection from any wind which might rise up, and proceed to play cards from morning until night, with breaks only for the issue of the daily bread ration and its ritual sharing out.

The days were helped along by the fact that quite often we had something to smoke. After an issue of Red Cross parcels we could sparingly have a cigarette, rationing ourselves out because we never knew when or if another ration was coming along. The practice was usually to light up and smoke about half before snuffing it out and putting it back in the pocket or in one of the John Player tins which came with the British Red Cross Parcels, until one felt, much later, that it was time for another drag.

This time, however, one would smoke the "damper" down to its smallest possible size without burning the lips, snuff out the dogend and return that to the tin as well. There were cigarette papers about in the compound, and the tobacco from two or three of these tiny dogends could be removed from the nicotine-stained wrinkled paper, shredded together, although if they were fresh this could be a bit tricky because the tobacco would be sticky and treacly, and rerolled for further consumption. Even the dogend from a re-roll was saved for further rolling until the time came when there were only a few grains left from an issue of, say, fifty cigarettes, and then that was the end until the next parcel day, whenever that would be. By this time our little group of card players would all be in the same boat and whatever one had in the way of smokes did not go very far, either giving a drag to another group member or cadging one for yourself, which was given unstintingly among us whenever one got down to a no-smoke situation.

Our position near the latrine gave us a vantage point with regard to the water supply. The taps on a piece of board were always left on because we never knew when the supply would be turned on. Sitting near the taps meant that as soon as water started falling on the ground we would rush to try to fill our tins or put our heads under the flow before the word got round and hundreds of bodies descended in a mad rush.

Barefooted we would rush to the water and come away black up to the knees, because the water running onto the open ground made it into a quagmire of wet black ash.

Sitting in the sun and playing cards we would indulge in flights of fancy about the kind of meal we would most like to eat. Although we were permanently hungry, this did not seem to cause any hurt at all and we never did tire of hearing what the food cooked by our mothers tasted like. Sunday lunches at home were most often trotted out as being the pinnacle of our desires.

It was not exactly an intellectually stimulating experience. We had nothing beyond a pack of cards to entertain us, absolutely no contact with the outside world nor anyone in it, no books, news, mail, nothing.

It was as if we were marooned on a desert island and a small one at that. But what we did have was conversation, and as we played cards for hours on end, so we told stories to one another. The stories usually concerned food, which was always the foremost topic in our minds.

We were all familiar with a tinned product called "Passing Cloud". This consisted of herrings in tomato sauce in an oval shaped tin, quite large, and was a favourite with army cooks as an offering on Saturday and Sunday teatimes. These occasions were usually missed out by everybody, preferring to use the NAAFI or some other forces canteen for a "char" and a "wad". But sometimes, usually because of lack of funds, if one went along to the mess hall, one would find a room full of empty tables with an opened tin of "Passing Cloud" on each. It was considered by almost everyone to be revolting stuff, and at the end of the day all the tins were thrown into the rubbish bins.

On one leave I arrived home on a Saturday. The next day my mother said she was preparing a special delicacy for teatime, something she had been keeping for me for a long time. I made a point of being home in time for the meal, when she proudly carried in a tin of herrings in tomato sauce. The brand – "Passing Cloud!". It brought home to me the fact that we in the forces were much better off for food than civilians were, and just how wasteful we were. One thing for sure was that in my present predicament a tin of "Passing Cloud" would have been a great delicacy.

Another thing we talked about was "spud-bashing", an army pastime which was universally disliked. Whereas we had thought nothing of wasting food in the past, now the very thought of our irresponsible actions caused us a lot of soul-searching. When peeling potatoes was a group activity, where we sat around a dixie and tossed peeled potatoes into it until it was full, then the job was usually done quite thoroughly and well, with little waste. But there were other ways, thought out by authority, to get this unpopular task done. One of them was to order that each man had to peel three potatoes on his way out of the mess hall after breakfast. The army potatoes were often very large, red ones with thick skins, and the waste was terrific as we used to cut the peel off in great chunks so that only half the potato would be left, because potato peeling was considered a very demeaning practice. How we thought about those thick potato peelings now that we had so little food.

After the issue of a Red Cross parcel, or more likely part of one, we could let our minds wander to moments when we had really enjoyed a meal. I remembered a time when we were stationed in Yorkshire and took part in an exercise on the moors. We were out for a long time, sleeping rough, not washing for days on end. It was winter time and we kept ourselves buttoned up and balaclavaed for most of the time. Then it was decided that we should all have a hot shower. Our troop transport turned up and carried us off to Scarborough where we parked on the main road outside the public baths. There were only a limited number of shower cubicles which meant a long wait for those at the back of the queue. I was one of the first ones and I was soon back outside with my wet towel rolled up under my arm, sitting waiting in the truck for the rest of the platoon to join those of us who had managed to get in early.

It was a very fresh sort of day as we sat there with the canvas sides of the truck rolled up, letting a wind off the sea dry our hair. The whole place had a clean, scrubbed look which was enhanced by a marvellous clear light so that one could see for miles, in complete contrast to the heavy grey sky with its rain-swollen clouds which we had got used to on the moors above the town.

Just across the road was a small cafe. Most of us didn't take much notice of it but one member of our platoon, always ready to seize any opportunity, seeing that our truck was only part full, disappeared through the doorway of the cafe. After about five minutes he appeared, holding something in his hand. As he climbed up onto the truck we could see that it was a fried egg sandwich. The fresh sea air, the marvellous light and the hot shower had given an edge to my appetite and I was out of the truck in a flash and into the cafe. The woman who was serving seemed to be overcome by the demand for egg sandwiches as we crowded against the counter. I managed to get one, paid for it and went back to the truck. It consisted of two thick slices of fresh white bread with a hot fried egg straight from the frying pan in between. As I bit into it the yellow from the yolk broke and dribbled down my chin and soaked into the bread. I turned the sandwich over so that the bread on top could take some of the overflow. The fresh bread, the warm egg, being at the seaside, gave a wonderful warm glow to my insides as I quietly ate my way through every delicious crumb. I finished up by wiping my yellow yolk-stained mouth and chin on the rolled up wet towel.

Moments like that were only relived after the issue of a Red Cross parcel. At any other time the mere thought of it could be agonising.

So, all in all, the time passed along with just enough food to keep us going, water to have a wash, cards and beautiful sunny days that gave us brown bodies and long bleached hair. Then one day all the British and Canadian prisoners were called out of the compound and lined up in the football field to be counted and recounted until finally we were marched out of the camp and once again pushed into the forty men to a cattle truck situation.

Chapter seven

We were in the cattle truck for a day and a night as the train rattled very quickly across Germany. Then early in the morning we stopped and were shouted out to line up alongside the tracks, to be counted and recounted and then marched off in a long column until we reached the gates of a large barbed wire enclosed camp with the traditional watch towers dotted around the perimeter. We had arrived at a British Stalag in Görlitz on the Polish border.

Inside the camp we could see British prisoners waving to us as we sat for hours, impatiently waiting to get into some sort of organised situation where even food might be available. After being counted and recounted innumerable times, the gates opened, we were herded into the camp and lined up on the football field for further recounts until we were dismissed and the inmates of the camp descended upon us.

These were mainly British sergeants and sergeant-majors with almost all the other ranks out of the camp at various worksites. Most of the regular inmates had been captured in North Africa and had been prisoners for some time. Initially they had had a very hard time of it, particularly from the Italians, and they were slow to forget their ill-treatment.

There were, surprisingly to me, Italian prisoners in the camp, who were barely existing. A favourite pastime of the old desert hands was to sit in the sun, smoking a cigarette, watching the Italians in their unfamiliar uniforms shambling past. As they came to the end of the cigarette, instead of keeping the dogend and returning it to a tin for further rolling, they would throw it onto the sandy ground. The Italians would be watching like sparrows in the hedges of a garden, and would pounce upon the dogend, whereupon the old desert hand would put his foot upon it and grind it into the dust, grinning while the victim's big brown eyes filled up with tears.

Because of the regimental shoulder flashes on our battledresses it was possible to identify which part of the country we came from. Soon sergeants were questioning those of us who came from their part of the country about life back home, which they had not seen for years.

A sergeant from the South Wales Borderers, Johnny, a regular soldier who had been captured in the Western Desert, asked me where I was from. When I told him the town he asked which area, and it turned out that he lived just around the corner from my home. He was very kind to me and saw that I had something solid to eat before I went to sleep.

We slept in a very large hut with three-tier bunks, on straw palliasses with a blanket each, an unheard-of luxury. The bunks were fitted with bedboards, small planks of wood about six inches by thirty. Most of them were missing, and some people said that they had been used to make tunnels, but it seemed more likely that they were used to fuel the tiled stoves.

I did not get a lot of sleep that night because, as ever, when one had decent food one suffered with "looseness", and I spent most of the time rushing to the latrine. One time, being half asleep, I miscalculated and dirtied myself just as I got there. Feeling terrible I washed myself down with cold water by standing inside the washbasin which was a circular trough about six feet in diameter with a series of small sprays set in a circle and a large circular ring to press down to get the water to flow. This was very unpleasant, standing alone in the darkness in the early hours of the morning sluicing myself with cold water and hoping that nobody would come along and see what a fool I had made of myself.

Daylight came and Johnny turned up with a cup of tea. This was delicious after all the deprivation. I still had my arm covered with the piece of blanket. He took one look, went off and then turned up with an old battledress jacket and a needle and cotton. The jacket was far too large so I sat outside in the sun with my back against the wall of the hut, carefully unpicked the sleeve of the old jacket with a razor blade, did the same with the ragged arm of my own jacket and painstakingly sewed the new sleeve into position. I now had some comfort when the days were chilly and during the cold nights. My arm was now fully healed and looked good except for a yellow discolouration.

We were given soap, pieces of rag, razors, razorblades and pieces of comb. Soon we were shaved and cleaned up all over. We washed our underclothes and shirts and hung them up to dry in the sun. We had food to eat and cigarettes to smoke.

The camp was well-established and there was a library with a large selection of books on all sorts of subjects. There was a camp theatre and a barber who would give you a haircut for a couple of cigarettes. The parade ground was used as a football pitch and we were lucky enough to see a football match during our short stay.

Even booze was made with the dried fruit from Red Cross parcels. One amazing object, also made in camp, was a machine for making heat to brew tea. It was on the principle of a blacksmith's forge, blowing air through charcoal to create tremendous heat which could boil water in no time. The whole contraption was made from the tins from Red Cross parcels, particularly the large Klim (dried milk) tins.

The machine was mounted on a bed board and consisted of a fan that was driven through a pulley from a hand wheel. The speed ratio was such that a tremendous draught was created through a pipe of cans into a container which held the charcoal. Once alight, and with the handle turning, water would boil in minutes.

Several of these machines were given to us by the old hands. Johnny gave me some tea, dried milk and sugar, so that in the mornings I could brew up a cup of tea for myself when I could lay hands on a "blower".

A ration of charcoal was issued to the camp for cooking purposes and as the blowers used very little fuel, it was always possible to get hold of some.

It was now early autumn and the mornings were chilly. The air was scented with the smell of charcoal from the blowers as small groups huddled around making their first tea of the day. Not that one could have many cups because supplies were scarce. The old hands had given up a lot of their stores to make us welcome.

Even in this organised situation savage fights often broke out. In one part of the compound several huts were occupied by French prisoners who went out to work each day and brought back into camp all sorts of food including eggs, which they would occasionally sell for cigarettes.

There were also a number of French Canadian prisoners in our group, strong men with long black beards who had sworn not to shave until they were liberated. Naturally they were the first to get organised with the French for extra food and had regular orders, particularly for the odd egg which appeared now and again. One day a French Canadian turned up at the French huts for his ordered egg, only to find that another prisoner had got in first with a better offer of cigarettes and had disappeared with the loot. When the Canadian caught up with him in our hut later that evening, a fight broke out which resulted in the offender having the two most beautiful black eyes I have ever seen.

Someone told me that if you had been a wearer of spectacles, but had lost them while being taken prisoner, then the Germans would replace them. My eyesight wasn't one hundred percent and I had been fitted out with glasses as a recruit, not that I had ever worn them and they had languished at the bottom of my kitbag for years. But I thought I would put my name forward to see what happened. Anything to break the monotony of being fenced in.

Sure enough one day I was told to report to the main gate to find a fattish middle-aged German sentry waiting for me. Off we set into the outside world. With no means of communicating by speech, since it seemed he spoke no English and I definitely didn't speak German, he guided me in the direction he wanted by pushing and pointing. We strolled along in the afternoon sunlight, he appearing to enjoy the change as much as I was, along a rough track which led along the outside of the camp. This turned into an apple orchard and ahead of us I saw a German woman standing on a small ladder picking apples off a tree and putting them into a basket. I couldn't take my eyes off her, naively hoping that she would take pity on me and throw me an apple as we passed quite close beneath her, but no such luck. It brought home to me the fact that fresh fruit and vegetables were a thing of the past.

We walked along at no great pace along a country road which eventually led into an old German town of grey stone buildings where the optician's premises were in the centre. My eyes were tested, with the sentry present, which didn't take very long , and then we were back outside making our way to the outskirts of the town, me in my familiar position in the gutter, while he strolled along the pavement. Suddenly he grasped my shoulder, stopped me, and turned me to face towards the pavement. We were outside a beer garden, at least that's what I thought it was, with tables under trees occupied mainly by old men drinking beer from large glasses. Motioning me to stay where I was, the sentry disappeared under the trees, still carrying his rifle on his shoulder, without a backward glance.

I stood there in the gutter while the old men looked curiously at me, shuffling about from one foot to the other as I waited in the late afternoon with the sun shining on the dusty old town. Everything was very quiet and still except for the low murmur of voices from the garden. There was no sign of the war at all, with the sentry out of sight even less so, and I began to wonder how long it would be before I saw home again, or if I ever would. The sentry was away for a long time and my mind began to wander as I drowsily stood there, back to Newhaven and embarking for Normandy.

We had started to go aboard the landing ships in the late afternoon. Loading up was a slow business because of the heavy and bulky loads of equipment we were all carrying. It was difficult to get through the narrow doorways and down the steep steps to the troops' quarters. I was in the last section to get aboard and onto the deck of the ship. No sooner had I stepped on than the mooring ropes were cast off the bollards on the harbourside and we began to move slowly out into the English Channel. The queue in front of me was moving very slowly into the depths of the ship so I slipped off my equipment, put my rifle on top of it and stood gazing at the other ships moving along with us, some with barrage balloons riding high in the sky, attached to their decks.

Not being in any hurry to go below I became the last person on deck. I didn't mind this in the least, despite the fact that it meant that I spent the night, half dozing, sitting on the top of the steps with other men lining the steps below me. The quarters below were more than full up as we made our way across the Channel. I was standing at the stern of the ship. Since the decks were now clear of soldiery, a sailor appeared and began coiling up ropes. He was dressed in faded blue overalls with frayed sleeves and trouser bottoms, looking just like the grey denim jackets and trousers which we normally wore in the week when we were doing any sort of training. We were issued with a fresh pair once a week upon handing in our used ones for laundering. This continuous washing made them almost colourless, while every edge became tattered, just like the sailor's. His dress struck me because we were all kitted out in brand new battledress which we had only worn once before when we tried them on for size. They were probably the best uniforms we had possessed since we had first been issued with a best suit at our recruitment. The sailor was off to war in an old pair of overalls while we had never been so well-dressed.

The light was fading fast as I stood gazing out over the stern. The sailor finished coiling up a rope and stood gazing with me. He turned to me and said, "Take a good look at it, Taff, it'll be a long time before you see it again". I had only been idly gazing around me until then, but at his words I looked hard shorewards, just about able to pick out a low line of white cliffs disappearing from view.

Yes, it was going to be a long time, I thought, as I stood there in the gutter of the sleepy old town. The problem with being a prisoner of war was that one had no idea when, if ever, one would get out, not like a criminal sentenced to so many years who knew when he would be released. With my thoughts getting morbid I was glad when the sentry reappeared and we made our way back to camp.

We were settling into a new lifestyle which we knew could not last long. Sure enough one day we were lined up and issued with winter clothing. In my case this consisted of a French army cap, a cape-like French overcoat with a long single row of rusty steel buttons and a set of winter underclothes made from some sort of blue ersatz material, and a towel. The next morning we were marched out of the camp down to the railway station and packed forty men to a cattle truck once again. The floor of the truck was covered with straw. But we were learning fast. Thinking that Russian prisoners might have been the last occupants and that the straw might be infested, we stood up, jostling and swaying, as the train moved along.

Chapter eight

The train ran on all that day and into the night through featureless countryside, and then finally it pulled up in the dark in a siding inside a factory. We were in a sugar factory in Poland at a place called Maltsch.

Floodlights came on to light up the trucks, the doors were slid back and the guards hustled us out onto the platform to be counted and recounted. We were then marched into the yard of the factory where we were given clock numbers, had the clocks pointed out, were shown how to use them, and allocated to shifts. We were to work twelve-hour shifts – "days" from six in the morning until six at night, and "nights" from six in the evening until six in the morning, seven days a week. At the end of every two weeks we would work eighteen hours on the Saturday, so that a switch could be made from day work to night work and vice versa. This meant starting at six in the morning and working until midnight, or starting at midnight and finishing at six in the evening on Sunday.

This was a shift system that I had never heard of before and it sounded rather daunting. I had seen at first hand, two- and three-shift working. I knew that an eight-hour night shift was disliked by anyone working it, so a twelve-hour night, with the occasional eighteen hour shift, probably without a lot to eat, was going to be tough. I was no stranger to factory life because before I had joined the army I had worked in a large plant, but I had been a staff person in a white coat, working from nine until five, enjoying a subsidised three-course meal in the canteen, with freedom to wander about at will. And now here I was, a forced labourer.

It was now very late at night but surprisingly we were marched into a big dining room and seated at long wooden tables where we were given a bowl of goulash type food which tasted marvellous, hot and tasty. It was the best meal I had during the whole of my captivity and needless to say nothing like it ever happened again.

The food was served up by German women, the first we had seen, and they looked quite frightened of us. In previous sugar beet seasons the labour had been supplied by South African prisoners who had probably got themselves into a prisoner-of-war mentality before they arrived in Germany. But we were ill-dressed and unkempt, and had never been in one place long enough to get into a prisoner's state of mind. Most of us looked alike, with our old French army overcoats, long hair, many bearded, eating our food with a piece of spoon and drinking ersatz coffee from rusty Klim tins with a piece of wire for a handle. We were rough and we looked it. Not that we minded civilians being chary of us. We were used, as infantrymen, to being treated as second-class citizens by people at home.

Our brigade had consisted of three border regiment infantry battalions, one English, one Scottish, and one from South Wales. When stationed in Yorkshire, the whole brigade was located in one area, the centre of which was the seaside town of Hornsea. There were a whole series of camps. The accommodation varied from Nissen huts and evacuated schools to empty houses. Every so often there was a complete interchange of camps with one regiment moving out and another moving in.

We were comfortably settled in one detached company camp when the order came for us to get ready to move again. The camp was miles from anywhere, Nissen huts with camp beds, a cookhouse nearby where one could get water, and officers hardly ever to be seen. However, one turned up to lecture us on our move. It appeared that we were now moving into Hornsea itself and that there was a problem. The good citizens of Hornsea did not want us in their town. They didn't mind the Scots or the English, but they drew the line at infantrymen from South Wales. We were given dire warnings about our behaviour. It appeared that people were afraid that we would be falling out of the pubs late at night and making a nuisance of ourselves by disturbing the peace by fighting or making our way, singing loudly, through the streets. Anyone would have thought that Gengis Khan and his hordes were about to fall on them. They must have seen too many daft films about South Wales, or were still living in the time of Wellington when he said of his army in the Peninsular War that they had only joined for the drink.

In fact, we were mostly young men, all volunteers, who rarely went into a pub except on leave, partly because we had no money and also because we had other interests such as watching rugby league matches or going to the pictures, which soaked up what little spare cash we had. We weren't keen on moving into the town anyway. We would avoid the centre like the plague because we knew that the main streets would be thronged with officers who expected a continuous barrage of salutes, and regimental police would be much in evidence. We were also going to have to give up our well-organised, detached company camp and move into empty houses. There we would be sleeping on bare floorboards without even a stove to heat water for a shave. To add to all these misgivings we now had the knowledge that the people of Hornsea had a very low opinion of us. We wondered if they realised that we were preparing for the invasion of Europe and that we were prepared to lay our lives on the line, for their sakes as much as anyone else in the British Isles.

We rarely came into direct contact with civilians when we were serving with the battalion because we were usually training in remote areas. When we did meet them it was invariably brought home to us how little regard the civilian population had for us.

When we were stationed in Aldershot, just before the invasion, the ancient barracks became quite intolerable in the early summer heat. We were confined to barracks, with all our gear either loaded onto company trucks or sent back to regimental headquarters. With nothing much to do, people began to make a nuisance of themselves. As a result the platoon commander, a Canadian lieutenant, marched us out to the nearest golf course to spend a few nights under canvas. It was good to get away from the barracks and out into the fresh air which had been so much a part of our lives. We were allowed to move around the area so long as we did not venture onto the fairways of the golf course. This was a rule that the golf club had made – it was a wonder that they let us onto the course at all.

Wandering around the lanes, near where we were camping, we came across the entrance to the long driveway of a large country house. On one of the gateway pillars there was a sign which said "Forces Club". Three or four of us walked up the drive to the front of the house and knocked on the ornate door. After a while the door opened and a well-dressed, middle aged woman appeared. She looked down at us, short stocky footsoldiers in our grey denim overalls, tattered and threadbare, and asked us what we wanted. We asked if the club was open, whereupon she asked what nationality we were. When we said that we were British, she told us that the club was only for Americans and Canadians, and dismissed us without a backward glance. It made us feel really good to be "Soldiers of the King".

But Soldiers of the King we were. One day in Hornsea we were ordered to put on our best battledress, polish our boots, clean our brasses and embark on our company troop transports. Off we set to an unknown destination. We eventually arrived at an isolated aerodrome to find the whole division lining up alongside the runway. Tanks, trucks, artillery, infantrymen. All were there in one long parade, where we were told that the King was going to pass by in a sort of inspection and as a salute to us who were off to take part in the ultimate adventure. We waited around for a long, long time but were eventually called to attention as the Royal family including the two Princesses, not just the King, came slowly down the runway in an open-topped vehicle.

There was a lot of moaning about the length of time we had spent hanging about, but secretly everyone was pleased that someone seemed to appreciate what we were about to do. The opinions of ordinary citizens were of little consequence when the Royal family, at a dangerous moment in history, could take the time to come along and have a look at us.

The meal over, we were marched back through the factory yard and round the back of the factory to a three-storey brick building which turned out to be our barracks. We were to sleep ten to a room on five double-tier bunks, each with a straw palliasse. There was electric light, central heating from radiators and outside in the corridor a series of large stainless steel washbasins. I don't think that it had been built for prisoners of war, more likely for German casual labourers.

Hot water came out of the taps of the washbasins and for most of us this was a great luxury. We had only enjoyed hot water for washing and shaving when we were at home on leave, no matter what sort of billets we were in or where we were stationed. In winter, particularly when in Nissen huts with the washhouse just outside the sleeping quarters, usually a series of cold taps in a long line over a galvanised steel trough or maybe a tin bowl, with reveille in the early hours, so dark that the stars were still visible, one would stumble from the dimly lit hut to the outside, tentatively splashing icy water on one's face, attempting to shave in the reflection of a piece of broken mirror. If we were lucky we had water warmed by the iron stove in the hut if it still retained any heat, a very rare occurrence. I was lucky in that, being fair-haired, I could get away with a minimal scrape for first inspection, something which the dark ones among us couldn't manage.

So as far as living conditions were concerned, for the harsh winter we knew was coming, we would be better off than ever we were back in our old outfits. The central heating, in particular, was something that we wouldn't even dream of back in our battalion days. It was so warm in the rooms that we were able to take off our uniforms and sleep in our shirts over our underclothes. There was nothing unusual in this – ever since joining up we had slept in our shirts. Never in all the time I served in the army did I ever see a pair of pyjamas being worn.

We didn't have any blankets to cover ourselves but slept on top of the straw palliasses, made of a rough sack-like material stuffed with stiff straw. These weren't exactly feather beds but not much worse then many of the places in which we had to sleep in England. At least the rooms were warm enough to ensure that we weren't kept awake by the cold air outside, as we had often experienced back home.

In a Nissen hut, presumably because of the concrete floor, your bed was usually a cast-iron contraption where the mattress came in three sections about six inches thick, known as "biscuits". In Yorkshire the winter before the invasion was bitterly cold, and it was quite an art to contrive an envelope from the three army blankets we had been issued with. Into this you would crawl, still wearing shirt, pullovers and socks. You would then stretch your army greatcoat over the top in an effort to combat the icy cold which seemed to rise up from the floor itself. We had all been issued with long johns, a combination of thick woollen vest and long-legged underpants. These would have been sensible wear in the wintry conditions, but they were always held in derision and languished at the bottom of our kitbags.

When billeted in empty houses we had to sleep on the wooden floor.

We didn't get beds at all, and although it was somewhat warmer than in a Nissen hut, the hard floor didn't exactly make for a comfortable night's sleep and, no matter what the sleeping quarters, getting out of bed in the early hours of the morning was sheer purgatory. So in a way we were being quite spoiled by the warmth of the rooms after all the hard living we had experienced back home. As far as those of us who were infantrymen were concerned, a lot of our nights had been spent in the open, even in winter, when we were out training. Sleeping rough outside never felt as uncomfortable as the inside of a Nissen hut. It must have been the concrete floor that made those huts feel like the inside of a refrigerator, and the curved corrugated steel skins probably didn't help either.

On the morning after our arrival, at five o'clock, we of the morning shift were rudely awakened by the guards and lined up inside the factory to be allotted places of work. A German called out the jobs and the numbers wanted for each area, for which men stepped forward and were moved off. Whether they knew what the jobs entailed, I don't know, but a group of us didn't want to volunteer for anything that the Germans suggested. We were left there until the end, to be allocated to the dirtiest jobs in the factory. These jobs were probably left to the end deliberately, to teach awkward workers a lesson. There was one consolation, our workplace was very warm in contrast to the bitterly cold weather outside, so much so that we worked stripped to the waist, wearing only an old pair of underpants.

This wasn't my first experience of sugar beet. When we were stationed in East Anglia in the middle of winter we were transported to a small hamlet, with billets in a large barn, to help with the sugar beet harvest. Outside the barn there was nothing but a couple of cottages huddling into the flat landscape in the bitter cold alongside a frozen ditch, although it was quite warm in the barn. We were told by the company commander that we would be paid a small sum of money by the farmer for each day's work we did.

At first light next morning we were carried by lorry, on the flat roads lined by frozen canal-like ditches, to the middle of nowhere, to be dropped at one end of a field which was so long that the other end could not be seen with the naked eye. The landscape was flat, featureless and depressing, and all a uniform grey except for the frost crystals which clung to the upturned lumps of soil where the beet had been loosened by machine. We were issued with a sharpened hook, shown what to do by a farm labourer, and left to our own devices. The beets were supposedly loose in the soil but the weather was so cold that they were frozen solid into the soil. We had to dig one end of the hook into the top of the beet, pull it out of the ground, hold it with the left hand, chop the top off and throw it onto a pile that was collected every so often by a man with a horse and cart, which we had to help to load.

It all sounds very easy but the beets weighed at least twenty pounds each, great heavy things they were, frozen into the ground. Pulling them out was made even more difficult by the frost which clung to one's hands until they were red and raw. It was very tiring work, made even more demoralising by the fact that no matter how hard we worked the field was so vast that the end never appeared in sight. No-one seemed to be the slightest bit interested in what we were doing, so much so that when we stopped for a bite to eat at midday from our "haversack rations", a lorry was supposed to turn up and supply us with a mug of tea each. This hardly ever happened, and when it did the tea was stone cold.

Although we were naturally unhappy with this situation, the thought of some extra money at the end of the week kept us going. We had joined the army to fight, not to be farm labourers. Most of us found the work degrading, because we were all volunteers who had left jobs which we thought were much more important than digging up beet. We looked upon the work as an imposition by the authorities who had absolutely no consideration for our finer feelings and who treated us like slaves.

The end of the first week came, and with it an announcement that the farmer thought it prudent not to pay us as it was probably against the rules, and that he had donated a bag of apples to the company instead. The announcement continued to say that there weren't enough apples to go round so they had been sent to the cookhouse to see what they could do with them. I never did see anything of the apples – if the cooks had any sense they would have sold them outside.

We felt that we had been part of a confidence trick and the following week did as little work as possible. At every opportunity we broke off to take shelter in a wooden hut. So little work was done that the farmer openly stated that he would be better off with Italian prisoners of war. We heartily agreed with this and soon we were transferred back to the battalion station where we had a certain pride in ourselves as fit, strong, highly-trained infantrymen, not "swede-bashers".

In Poland, the sugar beet arrived at the factory in horse-drawn carts driven by Polish forced labour. It was washed and then fed into a long vertical rotating cylinder, the walls of which were studded with knife blades about nine inches long which chopped the beets into pieces. These were then boiled, the resulting liquid was drawn off and pumped through a series of cloth filters which were clamped together. As the gooey liquid was pumped, these filters would slowly gather a thick film of steaming hot, grey, mud-like sludge until they became clogged, when the liquid would be diverted to another set of filters. The clogged filters would be unclamped, opened up and scraped with wooden spades to clear the boiling mud. This slurry slid down chutes to hatches at the bottom, which was where I worked. After every "scraping", which was continuous from one set of filters to another, we had to push heavy steel drams, which ran on overhead carriages, underneath the hatches, open them up and let the boiling mud flow into the dram. When it was full we would push it along to a lift on the outside of the factory which hoisted it into the air and then transferred it to a long conveyor. This carried it away to be tipped onto a mound.

The area where we worked was like Dante's Inferno. Ill-lit, with the steam from the mud limiting visibility even more. We were supervised by a little old gnarled German worker, who although often exasperated by us, was not a bad old chap. He, like the rest of us, worked in a pair of undershorts and on his feet a pair of wooden clogs. These played havoc with our bare feet, so we covered them with "footrags" to try to make life easier.

Apart from the guards who regularly patrolled the inside of the factory with their rifles slung over their shoulders, the only other German with whom we came into contact was the man in charge of the filters, and of the prisoners scraping them, on the floor above where we worked. He was a dark haired young man, actually a member of the German army, released each winter to work on the sugar beet harvest. It seemed that this had to be done as soon as possible, and the factory kept running continuously once it had been started up. The workers above us cleaned off the mud from the filters with their wooden spades, and occasionally, particularly if they burnt their hands on the hot sludge, a spade would be let go, fall down the chute and into the sludge behind the hatch in readiness for us to do our bit.

Whenever this happened the young German in charge of the filters would come down himself and ask us to try to find the spade before it was despatched to the outside dump where it would never be found. He would indicate which chute held the missing implement, which we would then open up and allow the sludge to drop into the dram, a good half-ton of the stuff. It was a difficult and dirty job to retrieve what he was looking for. Initially we would look at the full dram and then gaze at him queryingly, as if inviting him to take a header into the gunge. But he wasn't stripped down like us, and had to stand back to keep the mud splashes off his clothes and to keep his feet off the slimy mess underfoot. But he was so polite and patient that we would relent, poke around in the sludge with a stick until we found the tool, wash it off and hand it to him. He would be profuse in his thanks and act in a very friendly way towards us, as if he wanted to associate himself with us as fellow soldiers. We couldn't see any point in his behaving like this, because all he had to do was to call in a guard and we would have been forced to do whatever he ordered. But it made a change to have someone acting pleasantly towards us, and in our condition we were thankful for any small mercies.

We were not very keen on working for the Germans and all sorts of minor acts of sabotage were carried out. One favourite was to put a large stone in with the beet as it arrived at the cutting cylinder. This would make a hell of a row as it whizzed round and would knock pieces off the knives so that they had to be replaced.

Underneath where we worked was a very long heated cylinder which slowly revolved and dried the residue of beet left after boiling. When this material reached the bottom of the cylinder, the hatch was opened and fellow prisoners filled sacks of it for use as cattle feed. Every so often the area where we worked would fill with suffocating smoke, and we would know that the boys downstairs had let the cylinder fill up and overheat so that it burst into flames.

Our German supervisor could not watch us for every minute of the day, and although armed guards were constantly patrolling, we had the occasional opportunity to do our own bit of sabotage. When the sludge was scraped into the steel chutes, regular emptying was essential. Each chute when it was opened would fill one dram, and we had to keep moving along the line of chutes at a fair pace. On the night shift, now and then we would bypass the odd chute, let the sludge inside settle, and not empty it until another load had dropped. When we did open it the sludge would be like heavy cement which would thump into the dram and meant that the load weighed twice as much as it should. We then had to strain every sinew to push the dram into the lift without the old German catching on. Once in the lift we would shout to the Polish operator to take the dram up. The lift would groan its way upwards under the extra weight. At the top the dram was hitched automatically to the overhead cable and we would watch as it disappeared into the darkness to tip its load on the large mound of waste sludge at the end of the conveyor. With a double load on board, the dram would gather a lot of speed. As it tipped its load, the excess weight and high speed would cause it to come off its cable and plunge out of sight into the filthy mess below. Normally, the dram tipped its load and automatically returned to the top of the lift shaft. The Polish operator would be waiting for our overweight dram to come back. He would be perplexed when it didn't return, and would halt operations all along the line until someone had gone out into the night to find out exactly what had happened.

On one occasion, when we were working a day shift, there was an air raid on Breslau during the previous night. When we were marched to our clocking stations it was about 5.30 on a fiercely cold winter morning. We were lined up and addressed by a German officer. He told us that because of the air raid, the factory was on emergency power, and that when we got to our place of work we were to start the equipment up in stages, to avoid overloading the emergency generator. Every man had a smile on his face as we marched into the factory. At six o' clock precisely, hands reached out and every power switch in the place was pulled simultaneously. This must have blown the emergency supplies, because everything went out including the lights. We were left blundering around in pitch darkness and it took several hours before work could start up, by which time German workers and soldiers had taken control of the switches.

The factory was laid out on a series of floors which were reached by steel steps with a grid landing on each floor. During the shift a large drum of ersatz coffee was placed on each landing for the workers on that floor. This was of course unsweetened and pretty horrible stuff.

Some of our fellow prisoners were working where the syrup from the sugar beet began to take shape as a moist brown sugary substance. The part of the factory where this was turned into real sugar was manned only by Germans, because of its value I suppose, but by squeezing the moist brown sugar in one's hands it could be turned into hard balls which were good to nibble at. When the ersatz coffee drums were brought along to the landings the first man who wanted a drink would automatically throw a couple of sugar balls into the dram to sweeten the mixture before dipping his rusty tin can into it. Unfortunately this sugar addition would happen again and again until the drink became like a syrup and so sickly that it was undrinkable. The Germans would never dream of touching the "sugar" at all and when they occasionally sampled a cup of fully sweetened coffee, then a great deal of yelling and shouting would take place.

For these and other misdemeanours we would suffer various forms of discomfort. We would be rudely awakened, pushed out of our sleeping quarters, lined up and stood outside in the snow for hours on end while the guards turned everything inside out. They never found anything as far as I remember, except bag after bag of brown sugar balls, while our ill-fed bodies shivered in the icy wind.

Discipline would also be tightened up. The guards who patrolled the inside of the factory were, so we were told, from the Russian front, wounded soldiers who were recuperating, and they were not a very pleasant bunch. Generally, they left us pretty much alone, providing the work was moving along alright, but after any trouble they would tighten up. In one corner of our workplace we had a plank raised off the slimy floor on a couple of bricks, and particularly on the eighteen-hour shift, one of us at a time would have a lie down while the others carried on with the work.

I was lying on the plank in the early hours of one morning, a few inches above the steel floor covered with its grey slime, dressed only in a pair of shorts made from long underpants, with wooden clogs on my feet, with one shoulder against the wall which was running with condensation, to keep me balanced. I was half dozing when through the steamy mist a guard appeared and before I could struggle to my feet he unslung his rifle from his shoulder and gave me a clout in the ribs with the butt. It seemed that for some reason discipline was being tightened up again.

The work was very hard and we were fed only with a fifth of a loaf a day, plus the ersatz coffee on the landings. We kept going by eating vast quantities of the brown sugar balls which seemed to give us quite a lot of energy. Twice during our spell at the factory we were issued with half a Red Cross parcel each, with all the tins punctured so that we were forced to eat the contents very quickly, but they were a welcome Godsend which kept us going.

Apparently we were supposed to be paid for our work. We never were, but in the early days every couple of weeks we were paid in kind. This consisted of a ration of cigarettes each. They were French cigarettes, Gauloises, in a dark blue thick paper packet of twenty, and we received five packets each. We couldn't believe such luxury and although the dark tobacco was unbelievably pungent we smoked ourselves silly. After a couple of weeks the largesse came to an end and we were back to scrounging a smoke whenever we could.

The old German in charge of us, who looked about seventy to me, smoked a pipe and initially we tried to cadge the odd "roll" off him. There was nothing doing, so we gave up the idea and would have to watch him filling his pipe and lighting up whenever there was a break from work. He always sat down well away from us so that at least we did not have the misery of actually smelling his tobacco smoke.

In one of the Red Cross parcel issues a tin of cocoa was included. As we had no means of heating water to make a drink we decided to give it to the old German in an effort to sweeten him up a bit. So at the end of one shift – he worked the same hours as us – we rather diffidently handed it over, and the move paid off. The next day at midday the old man's daughter turned up with his food. There was a bit of a panic because we were wearing only our makeshift shorts. These were alright in our steam-filled workplace but rather revealing in front of a woman, particularly as we had not seen one close up for a long time. The object of her visit was to have a look at her father's "slaves".

From then on, the old man eased off us and would even turn a blind eye while one of us had a quiet sleep, especially during the eighteen-hour shift, when he himself by the end of it looked like a walking Zombie. As long as we kept the work going, we were able to relax a little, and he relaxed too, in that he left most of the heavy work to us. We didn't mind this because he got to look so old and tired that we felt quite sorry for him.

By now it was bitterly cold outside with deep snow all round. The river which flowed near the factory was frozen solid with great blocks of ice jumbled one on top of the other. At the end of a shift we would put our uniforms and overcoats on over our filthy bodies and line up outside to be marched back to our billets. Having got there, we would strip off and wash ourselves down at the steel washbasins. This is where trouble would start if there was any friction, say between different regiments or between Londoners and Northerners, and fighting would break out. In grudge fights, one dirty trick was to wait until your opponent had stripped off and was standing there in his bare feet. An argument would be started, fists would fly and the poor victim would find his bare feet being stamped on by large Army boots until he fell to the floor.

Some of these fights were caused by stealing, particularly early on during our time at the sugar factory. When we were on shift, the living quarters were open to everyone who was off shift. This normally didn't matter because no-one had anything worth stealing, but when we were issued with the French cigarettes some of us hid the odd packet inside our straw palliasses by making a small slit in the seam at one end and carefully jumbling the straw around the spare packets. But this was of no avail because on our return at the end of the shift, much to our dismay and disgust, all the cigarettes had disappeared. Suspicions as to the guilty persons were usually well-founded and for any excuse, however slight, a fight would be picked, normally of the Army boot versus barefoot type. This was the only redress available, there being no hope of getting the cigarettes back, and no-one to turn to for justice. It was a case of every man for himself.

So the weeks went by and the winter weather deepened. Christmas was coming and the sound of gunfire could be heard in the distance. Discipline in the factory slackened off, there was much less evidence of the guards, and the workload decreased. The building where we slept had obviously been built onto the back of the factory after the main structure had been erected, probably when the Germans started to use forced labour. The result was that there was no direct means of getting from the sleeping quarters into the factory, and to get to our workplace we went out of the door, fell in on parade and were marched through the front yard into the factory entrance. There was one door to the billets, a heavy steel-lined affair that was only opened when a sentry was present, usually at shift changeover, so that we were never allowed out except to go to work. But sometimes now at the end of a shift when we returned, if we were a bit slow, then the door might be open with no guard present. On one night shift George and I managed to get a few hours sleep in, and by midday the next day we were up and about quite briskly, whereas normally we slept the day away until it was time to go back on shift. The door to our quarters had been open when we came off shift, so we had a look down the stairs and found it still open. We got dressed in all the warm clothes we could find, made our way down the stone steps, through the door and out into the open, into the outside world on our own.

The railway lines in front of us ran across the back of the factory, to the left past a covered platform where we had arrived on the first night and where the finished sugar was loaded in sacks into covered railway wagons. But we had been that way twice a day ever since we had started work. To the right was unknown territory and we automatically turned that way. We were initially in a narrow alleyway with the back of the factory on our right. Across the railway lines was a high wire mesh fence, behind which was the huge mound of waste sludge. As we strolled along, the alleyway opened up and we came upon a group of fellow prisoners who were working at a lime preparation plant where large lumps of limestone were being burned in a small tower heated underneath by a red hot coke fire. Someone said they thought the lime was used to bleach the brown sugar white. It was a very cold day and the open vista in front of us was covered by a good foot of pristine white snow against which the glow from the burning coke looked a very inviting cherry red. We stopped for a chat and a warm and envied their ability to make a cup of tea whenever Red Cross parcels made a supply available.

We couldn't stay all that long because the German in charge of the gang came along and was quite annoyed to find us there. He was middle-aged, a big vigorous man with a great shock of white hair and a Kaiser Wilhelm moustache twisted to a point at both ends. He seemed like a nasty piece of work to us but the gang working for him got on well with him and soon calmed him down. He obviously wondered what on earth we were doing mooching about on our own, and we moved off, but not too far because where the back of the factory ended, the railway lines along which we were walking opened up into a large junction with many lines moving out. We stopped and looked ahead to see a railwayman's hut , and we moved along the lines towards it. The hut was heavily tarred on the top and sides and when we tried the door it opened at a touch. We looked inside to find that it contained a variety of tools which were not much use to us. The roof section was made up of a large number of cross pieces and hanging from these were long, dark brown, dried leaves. We pulled some down to find that they were not fully dry, smelled them and concluded that they were tobacco. We took most of them and stuffed them into our battledress jackets. We then beat a hasty retreat back to the billets to find that our luck was in and the door was still open.

Stealing from the enemy was fair game as far as we were concerned, but we had taken quite a risk. We would no doubt have been severely punished if we had been caught, and this risk wasn't really worthwhile because when we came to smoke the stuff it was really horrible. This might have been because it wasn't fully cured, and we threw it away, but actually it was no worse than some of the other materials we had tried to smoke, about the worst of which was tea leaves straight from the packet, although a type of plant which someone said was used as a fertiliser was not much better, maybe that was why it was associated with fertiliser.

The work at the sugar factory eased off once more and then ceased altogether as the ground floor filled up with German refugees sleeping on straw. They had fled from the Russians, something which we looked upon with mixed feelings. It was obvious that something was going to happen to us, because there we were, prisoners of war, sleeping in bunks in heated rooms, while German refugees were sleeping in straw. But Christmas day came and went and we were still there. The Germans tried to be festive and instead of a fifth of a black loaf they issued us with a little sweetened loaf made of white flour. This, unfortunately, was nowhere near as nourishing as the normal mouldy black bread.

There were ten of us in our room and one was "religious". How his religion had survived the army I'll never know. Any religious sentiment I had possessed on entry was soon quashed. It started from the moment you filled in your first form. The question of religion was soon glossed over and unless you firmly stated your religious tendencies you were automatically classified as Church of England, C of E, as if the whole question was of very little significance, and was just a matter of sorting people into C of Es, Roman Catholics (RCs), and other denominations (ODs). The latter category was much discouraged and Baptists, Methodists and the like were lumped together as C of E, unless the individual was very firm in his beliefs.

The next rude awakening came at the recruiting depot and the first Church parade. This was compulsory on a Sunday morning and required a lot of spit and polish to prepare for the inevitable inspection. Church Parade was used as a part of disciplinary indoctrination, as much as any other activity. We assembled on the barrack square and fell into three ranks, with the C of Es taking the prime position, the RCs and ODs falling in on the left. This being the first Church Parade we had experienced meant being herded by the training NCOs with shouts of..... "C of Es on the right, RCs and Odds and Sods on the left!" accompanied by their usual foul army language. This came as something of a shock to those of us who were expecting a more dignified and reverent occasion. Once we were in three ranks, the RCs and Odds and Sods were given the order to fall out and make their own way to their respective religious services. We envied them because we had to stand and listen to the shouts of the NCOs telling the C of E men to stand fast. We were then inspected, and we could just as easily be put on a charge as during any other parade, for crimes such as dirty cap badge, boots not highly polished enough, and other faults, before we marched off to the service. My feelings for the Church melted away by the minute.

I had attended church regularly as a boy, at my mother's insistence. This had dropped off after I left school, but I kept my respect for the

Church's activities, especially the work they did with people who were suffering during the depression of the thirties. Most of this work was carried out by curates, very active young men, themselves as poor as church mice. It came as a shock to encounter army Chaplains, dressed in their officers' uniforms, part of the officer class and hopelessly divided from the rank and file which comprised the bulk of the British Army. They had to be saluted, too, and one could as easily be put on a charge for not saluting a Chaplain as for any other officer. Some of them even seemed to enjoy the occasion and would give you a sharp reminder if you were not quick enough raising your hand to your forehead.

Saluting officers was always considered a bit of a bind and as far as possible one avoided them. This included Chaplains and I never spoke to one during my whole military service. Once I was in the battalion there was very little religion except for one Church Parade in Hornsea which was held mainly to reassure the civilian population that we were in fact human beings.

So I had had "religion" knocked out of me, but not this man – he used to get down on his knees before getting into bed and say his prayers, much to our embarrassment, and consequently no-one was particularly friendly with him. Now cigarettes were worth their weight in gold at this time. None of us had had a smoke for weeks, and for a packet of ten you could get a whole loaf from a Polish forced labourer, so that everyone had traded away their smokes for food. Our "religious" room mate was a non-smoker and as hungry as the rest of us, but on Christmas morning he produced nine packets of Craven A cigarettes and gave us a packet each. There's always something nice about Christmas, even if at times it can be embarrassing.

So Christmas came and went as had my twenty-first birthday way back in August, two occasions which I would really have enjoyed if I had been at home. Christmas in the army was a time that you looked forward to for weeks. The mere thought of Christmas leave was enough to gladden anyone's heart. The reality of being home in wartime Britain was not as rosy as in pre-war days and the real enjoyment came from the expectation of the leave. The Christmas before, the battalion was on an exercise in the Yorkshire Wolds for about a week, sleeping in the open and generally roughing it so that the thought of Christmas was made even more enjoyable. The exercise was due to finish on the day before Christmas Eve when we would be transported back to our billets to wash, change and then be taken to the station to catch our trains home. The exercise ended and the company paraded in a large field to wait for our transport to turn up. Wait we did, for a very long time. Our transport was held up somewhere and the time of our trains' departure grew closer. Frustrated, for the first and only time, we began singing together as a company, to the tune of "O Come All Ye Faithful", we burst into "Oh Why Are We Waiting". We were allowed a couple of choruses until the wrath of the discipline makers descended upon us and we soon shut up. Before we could get into real trouble the transport arrived and we were quickly on our way.

With Christmas behind us and nothing to do, with the Russians obviously getting closer all the time, we expected to be moved out at any moment. One day we thought that we were definitely on our way when we were all told to parade outside, but to leave our belongings behind. We fell in in column of threes and the whole working party was marched around the side of the factory into the front yard and then onto the road outside, somewhere we had never been before. We marched along for a time and then we were joined by a number of civilians who turned out to be Poles, young men and women, some of the latter were attractive, particularly so to eyes that hadn't seen a woman close up for months. They all seemed to be quite cheerful and very friendly to us although there was a big problem with the language barrier. Before we could become well acquainted, and hopefully find out what was going on, the corporal, who had come from the factory with us, came down the ranks telling us in a quiet voice to stop in our tracks. The Poles, who had filled up the roadway by walking along the fringe of our column of threes, looked bewildered for a moment, but then moved along until we were left on our own in the middle of nowhere.

We stood there for some time, when the corporal reappeared and told us that we were moving towards an area where a defensive position was being prepared against the Russians, and that we were going to be used to dig trenches for the enemy. Our corporal was having trouble with the Germans and told us to stand fast while he tried to convince them that it was against the rules of the Geneva Convention for prisoners of war to be used against their will in performing acts which helped their enemies. We were all very vague about this and we doubted whether the Germans would take much notice of the Geneva Convention anyway. As far as we knew, they had only ever paid lip service to it. The corporal stood his ground courageously, and we continued to back him by standing still in the roadway until eventually the Germans gave way. We about turned and were marched back to the sugar factory.

The noise of gunfire was quite audible by now and we knew that we would soon be on the move again. The corporal with our work party began to issue out all the spare kit which he controlled and I managed to get a new battledress and pair of boots. Stuff was appearing which we didn't even know existed.

The door of the billet was open all the time now and we could wander around as we pleased. One day George and I thought that we would have a look at the German civilians who inhabited the ground floor with its layer of straw, two or three feet deep. Perversely, we thought that we should look our best when we inspected them in their misfortune, so I put on my new boots and uniform, George tidied himself up, we borrowed a couple of British Army forage caps and then strode around to the main entrance.

The front yard had in it a number of empty carts of typically German design with canvas covered tops stretched over hoops, looking for all the world like covered wagons from Western films. Inside the factory, on and in the straw, were a large number of civilians including women and children. Tethered along one wall were the horses which had drawn them to this austere resting place. George and I had a quick stroll round, with the refugees staring curiously at us. Tidied up as we were, we looked a lot better than most of them, particularly the women and children. We didn't feel at all sorry for them because of the way we had been treated – being half starved is no joke. We strode out in military style, my new boots with their unmarked studs making a fine marching sound on the concrete floor.

The refugees probably complained about us rubbernecking them, because the next day the door to the billets was locked again and we were told to stay put.

It was shortly after that when, one morning, we were told to get ready to move and we dressed up in all the clothes we had. I put on my two battledress suits, one over the other, and pulled on my new boots. We were paraded in the factory yard and marched out into a field covered with thick snow just outside the factory. It was quite a sunny morning and just as well, for we were kept there for a long time until we were issued with one Red Cross parcel between two which we shared out and stowed away in our clothing.

Then we were lined up on the road, guards took up their positions on each side of the column, two open carts drawn by oxen took the lead, and we were on our way. Wherever we were going, it looked as if we were going to walk there.

Not that the thought of marching worried me in the slightest, an ex-infantryman, and because of the Red Cross parcels and a never-ending supply of brown sugar balls I felt fitter than I had for some time. Not as fit as in the days back in England when route marching was part and parcel of our lives. In Aldershot, before we moved to the coast, we were stationed in old barrack blocks with thick walls which retained the heat. It was quite a hot early summer, with smelly urinals at one end and very little light or air coming in. The barrack square was covered with our transport, loaded up ready for the move, and we were very limited in the activities we could take up. And so the twenty-five mile route march came into its own, I suppose in an effort to keep us occupied, to use up our surplus energy and to keep us out of the barracks as much as possible during the day.

Our normal route usually described an enormous circle around Aldershot. Unfortunately this took us through built-up areas and tended to inhibit us from singing our usual ribald songs. The longer the march went on the hotter our feet became, the sweat would roll down our faces from underneath our steel helmets, the small packs on our backs would cause our shirts to become sodden and our shins would ache where the gaiters pressed against our legs. One could also suffer from a complaint called "Hot Bearing" which was a steelworks expression used for overheated rolling mill bearings – quite a lot of the battalion had worked in Ebbw Vale steelworks before the war. This was a very painful misfortune and was caused by a sweaty bottom being rubbed by too tight denim trousers, which as they were dished out on a take it or leave it basis, did not always fit too well. My own main suffering was from sore shins. My feet, like the rest of the platoon's, were hardened after so much marching so they were no problem.

After about fifteen miles one would begin to feel the discomfort and it was then that we would begin singing marching songs to help us on our way. The words of the songs were always less than clean, which seemed to help us along, as they would always raise a grin or two. The trouble was that whenever we got into full swing, with the whole platoon giving voice, we would enter a built-up area and barked orders from the platoon commander, sometimes an officer but more usually a sergeant, would tell us to shut up. To enforce this was easier said than done, particularly if the song was a good juicy one, and it needed a lot of shouting and yelling from the platoon NCOs to get us in some sort of order. It could usually only be done by ordering us to march to attention, which meant getting our rifles in the slope arms position and marching with swinging arms, with our bodies in a stiff position. After a twenty-five mile route march one felt a bit tired in the evening and would sleep like a log, but the next morning one's feet might be a little sore, but otherwise there was nothing at all to worry about.

Another bit of torture which we had to endure was an exercise of ten miles in two hours which someone in the higher command had dreamed up. This entailed a series of running and walking interludes over ten miles which had to be accomplished in two hours. This started when we were stationed just outside Hornsea in Yorkshire, unfortunately in the heat of summer. We started the programme for a couple of weeks running and walking in PT kit, including soft shoes, and in our very fit condition found it no bother at all. Then we progressed to doing it in uniform with our boots on and again found it no problem. This was followed by attempting it in full kit, steel helmet, equipment, rifles, the three platoon Bren guns, mortar and the PIAT gun with its heavy case of projectiles.

We ran as a platoon in a tight column of threes, our heavily studded boots beating out a steady pattern on the tarmac as we ran in step for the required distance and then switched to marching for the same length of time. Even as we ran, we passed the heavier weapons from one to another to ease the strain and even broke them down into smaller pieces such as taking the barrel and other parts off the Bren and passing them around. Some of the older members of the platoon found this exercise particularly hard going but after a few weeks we got so used to the idea that we managed it quite comfortably, so much so that it was nothing after one of these runs on getting back to camp, to have a shower, cold of course, and then go out for the evening as fresh as a daisy.

So the thought of marching off somewhere didn't worry me at all.

Chapter nine

By the time we started it was early afternoon. The sun had disappeared behind low cloud and the first few flakes of snow were falling. We were walking through a flat plain, huge fields where potatoes and sugar beet were grown, on a narrow snow covered road which soon became obliterated as the wind got up and the snow turned to a blizzard. The way ahead was only obvious by wooden posts sticking up in front of us every fifty yards or so.

The snow as it fell was like flour and as we marched through it, a hundred or so of us, it trickled back into the marks of our footsteps so that on looking back there was no sign that anyone had passed that way. It became increasingly difficult to walk along, what with the deep snow, the howling wind and the fact that we weren't particularly strong because of lack of food. We were forced along by the guards for hours on end until it became almost too dark to see where we were going. When we finally stopped it was at a deserted farm. I imagine that the occupants had moved on as refugees. We were pushed into a barn that had seen better days, with the roof letting in the snow in places and the wind howling through gaps in the wooden walls.

The floor was covered with quite a thick layer of straw on which we settled and had a bite to eat from our Red Cross parcels. As it became really dark we curled up deep in the straw to try to get the chill out. In my ignorance I took my boots off, used them as a pillow and fell fast asleep.

I awoke in the morning to shouts from the guards who were kicking people to their feet, to find that my boots were on top of the straw and frozen solid. As I reached for them I found that I had been sleeping all night next to a dead horse. I had a terrible struggle to get the frozen boots on before I was bumped by the guards, and that was the last time I took them off for many a long day. I shuffled out onto the road where the carts with their oxen were already waiting and fell in to be counted two or three times. This gave me a chance to have a morsel of food from inside my battledress blouse and to stamp up and down in my boots until they thawed out a little and I was able to tie the laces. Then we were off on the road again, in a rough column of threes, with the ox carts leading and the guards marching alongside every ten yards or so. The storm of the previous afternoon had passed and as we marched along the road slowly became clear of snow.

We marched along side roads in the main. At one point we passed a halted tank column crewed by SS troops in their black uniforms with silver ornamentation. They looked arrogantly down on us, sneering at our misfortune. This was annoying enough but what made matters worse was that tied on the back of each tank, behind the turret, was a large plywood box of British Red Cross parcels. There must have been at least fifty parcels in each box, and to think that we had never had more than half a parcel each at any one time, and even that very rarely.

We kept marching all that day. Luckily it did not snow, but as the light faded it became bitterly cold. We kept moving along at quite a brisk pace, for we were in relatively good shape, which was just as well considering what lay ahead.

That evening, in the half light, we came upon a covered wagon train halted by the side of the road. There were women and children aboard, with men standing at the heads of the horses in the bitter cold. As we passed by we asked these refugees in loud whispers whether they thought that war was good. And so into another barn for the night. It appeared that we were making our way towards Görlitz, back to the Stalag which we had set out from, marching all day and sleeping in barns at night. Our Red Cross parcel supply soon ran out and we started to exist on the fifth of a loaf ration. Some mornings before we set off we were issued with a drink of unsweetened ersatz coffee which by the time we received it was invariably cold.

One day we were aroused earlier than usual with a lot of commotion and excitement from the guards. When we lined up to march off we found that we had changed direction and were now heading away from Görlitz. Someone said that the Russians had started to probe in that direction. Going off the other way, we arrived at a prisoner of war camp in a place called Sagan. This was now deserted but had been a Stalag for Airforce prisoners who must have been moved out of reach of the Russians. This was the camp where we had heard that a mass breakout attempt had been made, and in retaliation the Germans had shot a large number of the flyers on their recapture.

We were herded into the camp and left to our own devices. We explored the empty huts, many of which had drawings and paintings on the walls, and helped ourselves to paperback books from the camp library. Then we found that there was still a little food in the camp kitchen, mostly a flour-like substance which didn't smell too good, but when you're starving hungry you'll eat anything. We filled the stoves with books from the abandoned library and soon had fires going to heat the porridge-style food. We slept that night on wooden floors in relative comfort and were surprised to find that we were not moving out on the next morning. We spent three days at Sagan in relatively pleasant surroundings. The ground was a soft yellow sand and the camp was surrounded by pine trees. During our time there, more and more prisoners arrived and were pushed into the camp willy-nilly. There were all sorts of European nationalities, many of whom I had thought were allies of the Germans.

After the three-day rest, in the late evening, cries of "Raus, Raus!" rang out again, and in the gathering gloom we were marshalled into our respective groups. The commotion was unbelievable as by the light of flares the Germans tried to count up their charges. People were moving about from one group to another and to add to the shambles a Canadian from our group had found a gramophone and a record which he kept playing over and over again.

Amongst the confusion a group of Serbs and Croats were trading bread for whatever anyone had to offer. They were dressed in grey uniforms and their overcoats and fur hats were in immaculate condition. God knows where they had come from and what they were doing there. The only thing which I had to spare was the new battledress which I had on under my old one and I offered this for a loaf of bread. It was accepted and there and then I stripped off, handed over my new clothes and put back on my old suit, the one I had landed in Normandy with so long ago, the one with the odd sleeve.

So, nibbling away at the mouldy black bread, George and I were swept through the gates of Sagan stalag along with the rest of our group, plus more British prisoners who had joined us.

The Germans were obviously in a hurry, which I presume was the reason for the night march, but our speed was largely determined by that of the oxen, so as the night wore on we slowed to a more sedate pace. Marching like this, through a dead landscape in the pitch dark, I began to imagine things, almost like having hallucinations, and occasionally would step over non-existent dogs and the like. We marched well into the morning before we finally landed up in another straw-filled barn.

The next day we set off again and now began a pattern which lasted for quite some time – marching about fifteen miles a day and sleeping at night in barns. Some of the farms were empty, and others still occupied. Each night we were issued with our ration of one loaf to five men, and most mornings a drink of ersatz lukewarm coffee. As the days wore on we became starving hungry and would eat anything we could lay our hands on.

We kept marching along side roads where we saw very few people, and kept away from the major roads, except that we would occasionally cross an autobahn. It was just as well that we were isolated because after a few days of marching from Sagan everyone developed stomach trouble. We were in an area where there was little snow and the sun even shone through occasionally in the daytime, but an icy wind always seemed to be with us. Every so often the column was halted for a rest and immediately men fell out on each side of the road and dropped their trousers. For toilet paper we used pages of the books we had taken from Sagan. As the guards shouted us back onto the road the wind would lift the soiled paper into the air and cover the countryside. Not very pleasant.

This complaint had a very weakening effect and some of us became very ill, but were forced to our feet by the guards and made to march on. After a while the epidemic wore off, but for weeks afterwards whenever we ate anything, we suffered with stomach trouble.

As the march went on we were joined from time to time by small groups of British from work parties along the route. Among one of them was a friend of George's whose nickname was Busty. He was an SAS man who had been captured in the desert, and was almost as wide as he was tall and strong with it. So now we marched three abreast and surprisingly our morale became quite high, so much so that we decided to bring up the rear of the column and try to help laggers. The rear was surrounded by a half circle of guards who would shift any stragglers along, usually with the butts of their rifles. These people were usually very weak from stomach troubles and lack of nourishment, and quite often it was the big tall men who fared the worst. At the rear of the column we would try to help them along and encourage them to keep moving and out of the clutches of the guards.

We spent the nights in all sorts of peculiar places. Once we stopped at an indoor riding school and slept on a peaty sort of surface. This place was deserted, and we seemed to be bringing up the rear of a mass evacuation.

The countryside we were moving through was sparsely populated at the best of times. Although we were moving mainly along secondary roads, back home we would have been bound to pass through villages with the distances we were covering. Here was only the odd small deserted farmhouse, and never a sign of anyone except ourselves. We must have been the last through before the Russians arrived, and they couldn't have been far away because of the speed with which we were being forced along at the insistence of the guards. This coupled with the fact that we were slowly starving to death wasn't doing our bodies any good at all.

Another night we arrived at a building after dark and were all jammed inside. It was a single-storey barrack room with a concrete floor. Down the length of one side was a raised wooden platform about six feet wide. This was occupied by a large number of Frenchmen. After about half an hour the French were called outside and immediately there was a mad dive onto the platform. Unfortunately I, with quite a few others, failed to get a place. The platform was jammed tight with bodies and so I spent the night in a crouched position on the concrete floor. It was bitterly cold with the ground frozen hard outside, and I was very glad when daylight came and we were back on the march again. There was something to be said for sleeping in straw after all.

One day we were marching along a major road for a change and came to a bridge over a wide river. The bridge looked as if it was wired up for demolition and there was no sign of any traffic. We went shuffling across in single file in the gutter, me in my broken down boots,

French overcoat with its single row of rusty buttons, old French forage cap, my rusty Klim tin hanging from the side loop of my coat, covered with bits of straw and odds and ends of accumulated dirt, unwashed and unshaven for weeks, looking worse than any tramp you've ever seen, half starved and showing it, when across the bridge, strutting on the pavement, came two young German soldiers. The clatter of their jackboots caused me to turn round and have a look at them. They must have been wearing their best uniforms, brand new and glittering with medals, highly-polished jackboots and gleaming healthy faces, so that I was amazed that anyone could look so fine. By now our guards were starting to look almost as tatty as us. In my astonishment I strayed out of the gutter and onto the pavement just as the two immaculate Germans approached, and was rewarded by a hefty kick up the backside from one of the highly polished jackboots, which soon brought me back to earth.

The snow still held off, although the fields we passed were thick with frost and it was bitterly cold. Somehow we kept going on our fifth of a loaf a day. One day we didn't even get that. We were pushed onto the road as usual, though, and set off again. As the day wore on we marched through a more than usually barren landscape, although this may just have seemed so because of our extreme hunger. Then we stopped for a rest where the road ran along the back of cottages in the middle of nowhere. Immediately the three of us slid over the wall to find a sand-filled box with carrots in it – a carrot clamp! There wasn't much in the clamp, but enough to stuff a few in our battledress jackets, climb back over the wall and get back on the road again. As we marched along we munched on our carrots and polished off the lot. This was a big mistake, because our poor old stomachs couldn't take it after becoming accustomed to a fifth of a loaf a day. We were soon dropping our trousers at every halt, to disgorge pure carrot!

That night and the next morning again we didn't get any bread ration. We were on the road in the morning and on our way in a pretty desperate condition. For the third day we received no food but were kept moving. It was a grey time, the skies overcast and menacing with low hanging clouds. Flurries of snow and a bitterly cold wind cut through our increasingly threadbare clothes. We were kept marching until it was almost dark and finally came to a village with a brickworks on the outskirts. It was the first time that we had been in anything bigger than a farm since the march started, and hopefully after three days without food we thought that we might be lucky.

We were pushed into the brickworks in the pitch dark and looked around for somewhere to sleep. The ground floor was just earth covered with a very thick layer of brick dust, so we opted for the next floor which was made of slatted wood. As we sat down with our backs against the wall, clouds of brick dust began falling from the slatted floor above, which we found was occupied by French prisoners. All the floors of the building were made up of open slats with thick brick dust everywhere. Each time someone above you moved, you were doused with choking dust. Shouting up at the French made no impression, and we just had to put up with it.

A light appeared on the ground floor and it appeared that we were to have soup. It had been a long time since we tasted soup, but knowing how unappetising and watery it would be, we weren't particularly excited, although after three days without food we were ready to eat anything. Down we went into a sort of Hell's Kitchen. One of the German guards had a ladle over a large drum of soup which he was doling out by the dusty light of a sort of naphtha flare. I lined up and held out my rusty Klim tin to have it filled with a piece of swede and hot water, that's all it was. However it was hot and I drank it down and munched my piece of swede so that it filled my belly out a bit. The air was full of brick dust from the movement of people on the floor above. The light from the flare cast only a limited semicircle over the soup drum and outside that it was pitch dark. I had only moved a few yards before drinking down the watery soup, and noticing that there was only the one German ladling out and no-one else about, joined the queue again, drank my tinful and rejoined the line. I did this four or five times until finally the guard recognised me but even then he only waved me away with his ladle. I think that he felt sorry for me. By the end of it all my stomach was fully distended, not that there was any nourishment in it, but at least I fell asleep on the slatted floor that night feeling that I had a full stomach.

Before this happened, however, the French prisoners on the floor above, whom we had been berating for bringing dust down upon us, were called out by the guards. Immediately we were up the stairs to find a better place to sleep, only to find that the French weren't exactly leaving because their belongings were still there. We had nothing at all, a rusty tin and a spoon at most, but the French had been prisoners for a long time and had acquired possessions. This was too much for some of our number who began to ransack the packs and suitcases left behind. They took items which they felt like or needed, like spare boots and jackets – clothing, mostly. Luckily for the French they weren't outside for very long, but when they returned all hell was let loose when they discovered that they had been robbed. In the dark that night the brick dust fell on us in great clouds.

The next morning we fell in outside the brickworks and were marched off to the village square and lined up along one side. Again it was a grey dull day with lowering skies, the houses looked grey and so did the square. In the middle of the square was a long trestle table covered with bread, and we lined up one by one to receive a full loaf each from a German officer, the first of his kind that I had seen since the sugar factory. The villagers were out as well, on the other side of the square, all looking very unhappy, and even the officer looked down in the mouth. I never could understand the ceremony when we hadn't had anything to eat for three days.

When we had all received one loaf we lined up ready to march off again when there was quite a commotion, and we were kept hanging about for some time. This gave us the opportunity to break off pieces of bread for breakfast before stuffing the rest into our battledress jackets. Finally we set off down one of the village streets, only to find out why we had been held up. Lined up on both sides of the street were the French prisoners who had been robbed the night before. As we moved slowly three abreast past them, there were excited cries as their belongings were spotted. The guards hauled the culprits out of the column, forced them to divest themselves of the stolen property and then clouted them back into line. It was good to get away from there.

The roads by now were covered with snow again as we continued on our way across Germany. The oxen were still pulling the open carts with the sentries' belongings, but they were starting to feel the strain, and one day as we moved along small red drops of blood began to appear on the white snow of the road. One of the oxen was beginning to fail.

The drops became bigger and more numerous and then one night we arrived at a farm after dark to be told that we were going to have ox soup. One of the NCOs got a fire going in an outhouse which housed a boiler for washing clothes. Pieces of the ox which had died that day were stewed up in the boiling water. After a long wait into the night we lined up and had a tin full of ox soup which was absolutely marvellous, and the sort of thing which kept us going.

Without an ox to pull one of the carts, prisoners were detailed to pull it along as we set off the following morning. For some reason we set off rather late and the march went on well into the night before we stopped at a very well-stocked barn, full of hay and straw, so that everybody sank out of sight to keep the cold out.

We occasionally had a day off from marching and it looked as if this was going to be one of them, because when I woke up and stuck my head above the straw the sun was shining and streaming through the open side wall slats, it was gleaming on the deep white snow outside. As I looked around to see what was what, a fellow prisoner came through the half open barn door. It was a comrade of mine from my old battalion who had been taken prisoner quite some time after me. He had been a despatch rider and one day he had got himself hopelessly lost so that he found himself way behind the enemy lines, with the inevitable result that he and his motorbike had been taken prisoner. As he passed by me I said "Hello, Griff", at which he stopped, grinned, put his hand inside his battledress jacket, and threw something to me. It was a packet of cigarettes, American, Camels. I couldn't believe it. It was weeks since I had had a smoke, and any cigarettes that were about were like gold.

So where had he got them? It appeared that he had been detailed with others to pull the wagon of the ox which had died, and during the evening as we trudged along he had got underneath the canvas cover to find a pile of American tobacco and cigarettes among the German soldiers' packs, which had come from American Red Cross parcels. He had stuffed his jacket with cigarettes and tobacco and slid out from under the cover without being spotted, which was amazing because the wagons were always accompanied by several guards.

It shook me to think that he had taken such a risk, because if he had been caught it would probably have been the end of him, and also to think that he had the generous spirit to give me one of the precious packets, it restored my faith in human nature.

He had been out of the barn to get a light, so I pulled a cigarette out of the packet and lit up from his. I had bedded down with a small group of about half a dozen, of which I was the first one awake. As I took the first drag and blew the smoke out in sheer ecstasy, heads popped up all around me like rabbits out of a hat. It was quite astonishing. I handed the packet around and soon we were all smoking like mad.

It was amazing what it did to the morale of our little group, and as we were not marching that day we for once had quite a pleasant time, with the sun shining out of a clear blue sky onto the deep virgin snow covering the countryside. Although it was cold it was a fresh, sharp cold which wasn't felt if one moved around. As far as hunger was concerned we had reached a state where we only expected enough to keep us barely alive.

The farm was occupied and very prosperous looking. Things were obviously beginning to change. We had been weeks walking through a grey, desolate, almost uninhabited landscape and now there were signs of life other than our own, although we still had to exist on our five man to a loaf ration.

The next day we set off again and then stopped for the night in a village where we were herded into the village hall. This actually had electric light, which was the first we had seen since the sugar factory way back in December. We were obviously getting into a more civilised part of the country. At one end of the hall was a stage with curtains. Busty, George and I soon had them torn down for use as blankets. What a luxury to sleep in a proper building, although the wooden floor was rather hard.

We carried on marching by day and sleeping in barns by night. One day we stopped at a very large farm. The farmhouse was huge and the barns even bigger, while the cobbled farmyard was like a parade ground. We had acquired a German sergeant-major from somewhere who turned up on a bicycle. He got us all lined up in front of him in the farmyard and gave us a lecture about stealing. The farm was still occupied and working, with all sorts of livestock. We had set off very early that day and had arrived at the big farm by midday, so we had time for a good look round. The German sergeant-major was a huge man, about six foot six with big feet. On the small platform over the rear wheel of his bike he had tied a cardboard box containing a brand new pair of boots. As he was lecturing us he had left his bike leaning against the wall of a barn facing the ragged array in front of him, so that several hundred eyes were focussed on his belongings. Sure enough in the mêlée that followed our dismissal after the lecture, someone stole his boots!

When things had settled down we had another look around the place. Some of us gathered bits of wood and several small smoky fires appeared. At this, the farmer came along, waving his arms about, shouting at the top of his voice and dashing about the farmyard kicking the smoky fires to pieces. He was worried about the smoke attracting the attention of enemy aeroplanes. For some time now we had been existing in a world which had no evidence of war at all, except for the lack of people. Now suddenly we became aware that the war was still on with a vengeance. From then on no-one ever attempted to light a fire of any description.

Mooching around the farm we came to a long low barn with an open door. Inside against one wall was a row of cattle stalls occupied by cows munching from troughs. It was peculiar to see animals being better looked after than we human beings. The barn was separated in half along its length by a low wall about eighteen inches high, which kept the cow dung clear of one half of the barn's cobbled floor. The building was about thirty yards long and right at the end, in the clean half, was a huge pile of very small potatoes, probably for use as cattle feed. Animal food or not, they would do us in our starving condition. But there was a snag. Inside the barn was a German soldier, but he seemed to be more interested in the cows than in keeping an eye on the potatoes.

After a short discussion I volunteered to get at the potatoes. I handed my overcoat to George, got down on my stomach and slid quietly around one corner of the wide open barn door. I quickly crawled to take cover behind the low separating wall. There was no sign from the guard that he had spotted me, so I slowly made my way, hugging the cobbled floor and keeping close to the low wall so that I was out of sight of the sentry, right to the end of the barn to reach the pile of potatoes. Quietly I stuffed my battledress jacket with potatoes, lying on my back with my back against the pile, and stuffed away until I could get no more in, listening all the while in case the guard spotted me.

Having filled my jacket, I now had the task of making my way unseen back out of the barn. If I were caught now with the potatoes on me, actually in the act of stealing, I would have been in deep trouble and the least I could expect was a severe beating. So I turned onto my stomach again and began the slow crawl back, hugging the ground. There was one problem – by being greedy and filling my jacket to the limit, I had raised my chest about six inches off the ground. This made my back level with the top of the wall. By slightly lifting my head I could see over the top, where luckily the guard had his back to me as he continued to watch the cows.

Thinking that it was almost impossible to get away undetected, I began to crawl back the way I had come, every so often looking up to see the guard's back. At one point, about half way along, I drew level with him. He was about ten feet away. He still didn't turn round and I quickly made my way the rest of the journey, slid out of the barn door, round the corner, and joined George and Busty. Breathing heavily, I came to the conclusion that the German must have seen me – it was almost impossible for him not to have – and that he had turned a blind eye to my misdoings. The same guards had been with us from the start of the march, and looked somewhat worn because of it. As the weeks had passed, they had got more and more easygoing, not that we ever had anything to do with them if we could help it, and kept as far away from them as possible. It may be that they had developed some sympathy for our us in our half-starved condition.

Having got the potatoes, we now had to cook them somehow. Eating them raw would be a last resort. We couldn't light a fire because the farmer had put a stop to that with his frenzied shouting. I had always thought of the Germans as disciplined people but they could be as excitable as Italians, on occasions which hardly seemed to warrant such outbursts.

It was a huge farm complex which we were in. Mooching about still further in search of somewhere to cook our potatoes we came upon a sort of tarred shack, the sort of hut which you sometimes see near railway lines. This was a lean-to up against the wall of a huge Germanic farmhouse. There was a stovepipe sticking up from the roof with smoke coming from it. We knocked on the door to have it opened by someone who didn't look German. The three of us crowded in to find ourselves in the company of a man, a woman and a little baby living in terrible conditions in the tiny shack. They were slave workers, probably Polish. They couldn't understand us, nor we them, but we gesticulated towards their woodburning stove and showed our potatoes, at which they nodded. We put the spuds straight onto the red hot embers. It was very uncomfortable for us in the tiny shack, so as soon as the potatoes were charred black we scooped them out, carried them outside and started to gnaw at them. The insides were barely cooked but hot, and we reasoned that eating the black charcoal on the outside might possibly help our looseness of the bowels with which we were all still afflicted. So we gnawed away and for the first time in many days our stomachs were full, so much so that we began to be able to take stock of our situation as we sat on a grassy verge with our backs against a barn wall.

When I had jumped out of the farmhouse way back in Normandy, my knees had taken a bit of a pounding and now after weeks of marching my right knee felt really painful. I pulled my trouser leg up to find that the knee was very badly swollen and tender to the touch. There was absolutely nothing I could do about it, and then it came home to me what a mess we were in. Obviously if you became really ill then that would be the end of you. A lot of prisoners had dropped out of the column as we made our way across Germany because they were too weak and feeble to carry on. The main reason for this was particularly severe attacks of looseness of the bowels. We never saw them again and God knows what happened to them. So I just had to put up with the knee problem and hope that it would not get any worse, although the condition of my boots was not helping.

I had left the sugar factory wearing a brand new pair of boots issued from the Red Cross stock looked after by our NCO. They were typical Army boots with the soles fully studded and thick iron tips on the heels. I naturally walk on the outside of my heels, and from an iron tip and a one-inch leather heel, I had worn away the heel so that the outsides were down to the upper and I was walking on wedge-shaped heels. I took my rusty spoon and, using the handle as a lever, prised away half the wedge which came away with nails attached. I turned it round and, using two pieces of stone, one inside the boot as a last and one as a hammer, banged the loose piece onto the worn area. Amazingly it worked for both boots and I finished up with level heels half the original thickness. It made an incredible difference and from then on my knee got no worse.

By the time I had finished the light was failing. The day had turned misty with lowering clouds and as the three of us mooched about, seeing if there was anything worth scrounging, we noticed how sick, weary and demoralised everyone was. Some of the people that we had seen a lot of at the sugar factory were lying about as if they had given up. This particularly applied to those we found on their own. Some of them even had potatoes which they had acquired from God knows where, but were so far gone that they were making no effort to try and get them cooked. With the three of us sticking together through thick and thin, we had not given up hope at all, and it was strange how we suddenly noticed the poor condition of those around us. They must have been deteriorating for some time but we three had been looking out for ourselves relatively successfully.

This was probably brought home to us by the location we found ourselves in. It was the first time we had stopped at a working farm, and we thought that we were entering a civilised area. This was not so. The more normal the world outside became, the harsher we were treated. The guards became more disciplined, our meagre rations stayed the same, and all this was happening as we were surrounded by the great dark stone walls of the farm building with a drizzle falling from a threatening grey sky. It was an awful place.

It was the sort of place that had an air of desolation and grief about it, very much as I should imagine, people say, exists in the glens of Scotland where massacres by the English took place. There was no doubt in my mind that something awful had happened there at some time. I sat on a small stone outcrop, near the wall in a sort of grassy cul-de-sac, to keep myself off the wet ground, with my back against the grey stone wall, and for the first time I wished I hadn't joined the army. Never before had I thought like that. I had put up with the spit and polish, the square bashing, the blancoing, the hard discipline, the rough living conditions, the route marches, the out in all winds and weathers training and the lack of money. I had moaned along with everyone else – the infantry was never happier than when it was complaining – but I had never regretted joining up until I had arrived in this, the first working farm.

There was no need for me to be there. The job I had been in was a reserved occupation which meant that I wouldn't have been called up and could have sat the war out comfortably at home. It had been very unlikely that I would have to go and that worried me when I was over eighteen, because the boys I had been to school with were starting to leave for the forces. Being grammar school boys they were mainly volunteering for the Air Force, sergeant pilots and navigators, which was the glamour boy service in those days, although as bomber crew their life expectancy was short. The streets of my home town were showing a scarcity of male civilians, their place being taken by American servicemen, and I began to feel a bit conspicuous as a young man in civilian clothing. I was not really out of place because of the number of merchant seamen that were about in those days. I was still very young, not old enough to be called up, but the adventure of going to war strongly appealed to me.

I toyed first with the idea of joining the Merchant Navy. A friend and I went down to the docks to have a look at the ships which had just come across the Atlantic, small, rusty and unprepossessing. Also the U-boats were sinking a lot of ships at that time which rather put me off, so the dark blue sweater which my girlfriend was knitting for me turned out to be the wrong colour.

I suppose that in my heart I would like to have been a glamour boy and an air-crew man like so many of my contemporaries. I had the educational qualifications but my eyesight wasn't one hundred percent, although it was good enough for me to be A1 in the army, and I knew that being air-crew was out for me.

I realised that I just couldn't go on as I was, and I had to join the millions already serving in the war. So without saying anything to family, friends or employers, I went to the recruiting office in Newport Railway Station, signed on the dotted line and was in the army. I had no idea what I was letting myself in for.

Chapter ten

The next day we were on the move again and on our way across Germany. The roads which we were herded along were secondary roads now, not the minor country roads we had spent most of the journey on. As we moved along the weather started to improve. We must have been well into March by now, not that we had the slightest idea of the date. We were coming into built-up areas. One day we even passed a German army barracks with soldiers drilling on the barrack square. We were driven along in tighter formation than before, and this was probably due to the presence of the sergeant-major who patrolled up and down the column on his bicycle. One day we marched for a lot longer time than usual and finally arrived at a small town as darkness fell. We were lined up outside a sort of sports complex with tennis courts behind us. Then began the process of counting us, a process which seemed to go on for hours and hours. Eventually after a final burst of frenzied shouting we were pushed into the confines of a tennis court which was surrounded by the usual high steel mesh fence. Not knowing what was happening we stood around in small groups until it began to dawn on us that we were to spend the night in the open. This was the first time that this had happened to us since we were taken prisoner. We had always had a roof of some sort over our heads and now, here we were, in an inhabited, so-called civilised part of Germany, being more harshly treated than ever. It almost seemed that we were just a nuisance to the Germans and they were hoping that we would die off and solve the problem.

We made preparations for the night by putting one overcoat on the ground and then the three of us lay down on it, pulled the curtain from the village hall over us and finally covered ourselves with the other two overcoats buttoned together, the buttons of one in the buttonholes of the other. It wasn't too cold a night as we lay there on the red surface of the tennis court, looking up at the sky. It was then that we heard the drone of aeroplanes in the night sky and realised that we were getting nearer to the war again, although whether they were Russian or Allied planes we could not tell.

The sky was overcast and in the distance we could hear the rumble of thunder and see occasional flashes of lightning as we pressed close together to keep warm. I was in the middle, the most comfortable of the three, although we agreed to swap places as the night wore on. We drifted off into an uncomfortable, intermittent sleep. Despite our half-starved condition, we never had any trouble getting to sleep. We were like animals who lie up if they are injured until they recover, except that we used sleep as a means of restoring some strength to our bodies on a daily basis. But on this night we had a rude awakening.

The thunderstorm which we had seen and heard in the distance had quickly moved our way, and we awoke to find large raindrops falling on our faces. Slowly the rain increased in intensity until it was bucketing down with thunder and lightning raging overhead. Being in the middle, my body was immediately beneath where the two top coats were buttoned together, and with George and Busty straining at the coats to cover themselves up, there was a large oval gap between each buttoned up spot, through which the rain streamed, soaked itself through our curtain and slowly saturated me. I began to moan about my predicament but I soon shut up as the rain flooded the tennis court and we all lay in several inches of cold water, so we were all in the same wet condition.

There was no point in getting to our feet because there was no shelter at all in the pitch black night, and at least as we burrowed our heads into the overcoats we could not actually feel the rain hitting us in the face. After an hour or so the rain relented and the ground water slowly drained away so that we managed to doze a little. Eventually a faint light appeared in the sky and slowly people began to get to their feet and move around to ease their stiffened bodies. We got up as well and stamped around, slapping our arms across our bodies to try and awaken some feeling in our limbs. As it got lighter we could see what a horrible mess we were in, all of us. The surface of the tennis court was made of a sort of red shale which had turned into a morass during the storm, so that we had been lying in several inches of red mud. In the early light of dawn we looked at each other in amazement. We were all covered in a thin red coating. Our hands, faces, hair and clothes were all a coppery shade of red, so that we looked a bit like Red Indians. I fished my sodden overcoat from the ground and tried to wring it dry but it was more saturated with mud than with water and as the guards began to shout for us to get on the road outside, I put the slimy garment on over my wet clothes and fell in with the rest of the column.

The last time that my clothes had been as sodden as this was way back in Scotland, in happier times. We travelled up from Yorkshire by train and after Glasgow puffed our way through beautiful scenery, at times up quite steep slopes on the sides of hills so that on looking out of the windows of the carriage all one could see was the tops of fir trees, so close that they seemed to be brushing the sides of the train. It must have been a normal service train because it stopped at every small station, some so small that the whole of the train could not possibly be accommodated at one go. In the hills the steam engine seemed to have real difficulty in starting off again without a great deal of puffing, heaving and the whistle of escaping steam. All in all it was a very enjoyable journey which ended at Inveraray on the side of Loch Fyne from where we were transported by truck to a hutted camp in the grounds of Inveraray Castle.

The huts were the familiar shape of Nissen huts with their semi-circular roofs of corrugated iron. But they were much larger than the ones we were used to, and another unusual feature was that the ceilings were criss-crossed with ropes, with three large pot-bellied stoves placed down the middle of the gangway in between the rows of camp beds. Straightaway we were issued with several pairs of denim fatigue suits and told that in all probability we would be getting wet every day, and that when we returned each evening our wet clothes could be dried by hanging them on the ropes above our heads where the rising heat from the stoves could get at them. Fuel for the stoves was in very short supply and we were warned of dire consequences if we attempted to cut down any of the trees from the woods in which the camp was situated. Such a possibility would probably never have entered our heads, but obviously the camp had seen a lot of soldiers and no doubt some enterprising souls had obtained fuel in one way or another. The warning itself gave a few of us food for thought which we would not otherwise have entertained.

The objective of our trip was to train us in the use of landing craft. Out in the middle of the loch, which was so wide in places as to be almost like an inland sea, a large troop transport ship named the Maracaibo was anchored. We were reliably informed that this had taken part in the landings at the invasion of Madagascar. Every day we were taken out in landing craft to the ship on which we would embark by climbing up gangways and then disembark by climbing down scramble nets hanging down the side of the ship, and thence back into landing craft which took us back to the shore near the camp for practice at beach landings. But it wasn't as easy as it sounds. In the first place the ship was very high sided, at least fifty feet from the top of the rails to the water below. The scramble nets were made of rope about an inch thick with meshes of about one foot square, invariably wet, and by their own weight pulled hard against the wooden top of the deck rails to which they were lashed. It was difficult to get a handhold as we were chivvied along in threes by NCOs from the deck and over the rails to begin the descent on the nets to the waiting landing craft below. With the slightest movement of the sea the ship would roll away from the net and then back, bashing us against its rusty sides, knocking our steel helmets over our eyes as we twisted our bodies to protect ourselves from trapping our rifles between us and the side of the ship.

There was always a delay before we reached the bottom, the nets would be swinging with the ship, the landing craft would be bobbing up and down and moving away to leave a wide gap of grey sea water before moving in again. This meant that it needed a lot of judgment to get on board, particularly for someone carrying a heavy weapon like a Bren gun. This delay meant that the men above you would start to stack up and close down on you as the NCOs on deck kept pushing men over the rails without a thought for what was happening below. Waiting for movement below you meant that you kept your two feet firmly placed in a mesh and your hands at head height gripping a horizontal strand. The trouble was that the man above you, looking out for his own safety rather than thinking about what was below him, was more than likely to place his heavily studded boots precisely on top of your gripping fists and then let his whole body weight rest on you, which caused some fearful yells until there was a readjustment of position.

We had practised with scramble nets before in Hornsea where they had been hung from the top of a disused incinerator just outside the town. It was a very tall building, much higher than the sides of the Maracaibo, and the funny thing was that we never practised climbing down but only climbing up, for some strange reason. Our first efforts were made in PT kit, then we progressed to denim fatigues and finally to full equipment including weapons. It was quite an easy climb in PT kit but there was some difficulty at the top where the nets hung over a low brick parapet about eighteen inches wide. It was quite tricky to haul one's body over this, and in full equipment, carrying a Bren gun, arriving at the top out of breath, with the weapon straining away at the muscles of your neck and shoulders, it was some feat of strength to get over. Just below the parapet the heavy weight of the net kept it pressed hard against the wall so that it was difficult to get a purchase and it was necessary to pause for a while before attempting the last bit of climb. You would wrap your arms tight in the net, gathering strength looking down at the long drop of the red brick featureless wall to make one supreme effort to get over the top, where some of the platoon were stationed to give a helping hand and words of encouragement so that the exercise could be completed.

The only thing about that sort of training was that it made climbing down the net, as we were now doing, seem a fairly easy operation.

Every day for a week we were ferried out to the ship to climb up a gangway, down the nets into the waiting assault craft commanded by pink-cheeked midshipmen of the Royal Navy, who would then proceed to put us ashore. But they must have been under orders to ensure that we all got a good soaking before we reached dry land and consequently they always beached their craft on one of the many sandbanks lying just offshore, with the result that when the front of the craft dropped down onto the sandbank it led as a ramp into quite a deep dip in the loch bottom, through which we had to wade. So every day we returned to camp soaking wet, if not from the sea then from the rain which fell constantly for the whole week. It was said that there was some sort of moisture in the air at Loch Fyne for three hundred and sixty-five days of the year, ranging from heavy snow, to rain, to fine Scottish mist, and we quite believed it as we hung our wet clothes over the ropes in the huts and changed into our dry battledress.

One day we finished early and a couple of us went for a walk down to the nearest inhabited dwellings. First we had a look into the pub, there appeared to be only one, but it was so uninviting that we didn't bother to go in, with just a bar, stone floors, no seats of any description and a couple of civilians who didn't seem to be enjoying themselves at all.

We then made our way to a small farm canteen, staffed by kindly Scottish ladies, to find that they were selling very thin Scotch pancakes at a farthing each. We couldn't believe our luck and with a cup of tea we bought six pennyworth of pancakes, twenty-four in all, which we demolished very quickly to the amazement of the ladies, who couldn't appreciate what a treat they were to us after army food, and the appetites we had developed with all the fine Scottish fresh air and exercise we were getting.

The day before the final exercise we ferried out to the Maracaibo in the late evening on quite a rough sea to spend the night in the troop quarters below decks. We lay about fully clothed and equipped, even as far as carrying live ammunition, on the bare wire mesh bunks in the holds. In the very early hours of the morning, while it was still dark, we were rousted out onto the decks. During the night a storm had sprung up, the wind was howling across the decks lashing the rain into our faces and the ship was rolling wildly. With some foreboding we clambered, heavily laden, over the rails and down the sodden scramble nets. The assault craft below us were bobbing about like corks causing long delays as men found it more and more difficult to jump from the nets into the boats. We clung tightly to the rope meshes as the Maracaibo rolled first to one side and then to the other, bashing us against its sides as it returned. As the movement downwards came to a halt so heavy nailed boots were planted on the bare hands gripping the ropes below. In the dark, with the rain lashing down, the wind howling past, and the clanging of weapons and steel helmets against the side of the ship, it was almost impossible to let the man above know that he was standing on your hands, hands which were already red and raw with the cold, and only by shouting at the top of your voice could you get them to move.

Eventually the assault craft was fully loaded and we set off up the loch in the dark. We were aboard for a long time, and when we were due to land, the first gleam of dawn was in the stormy looking sky. The boats were grounded a long way from shore, the front loading ramp went down and we filed out onto a sandbank which led us gently down into a dip in the loch until we were wading ashore chest deep in cold sea water with our weapons held above our heads to keep them dry. Once ashore, we were deployed lying down in the wet grass in straight lines and ordered to fire with live ammunition at supposed targets ahead of us, when a white flag appeared on top of the Brigadier's caravan which was slightly to one side of us. Suddenly the lashing rain turned to thick wet snow which completely obliterated the view in front of us. Nevertheless we kept firing until there was a frantic rushing about by NCOs behind us, shouting and yelling for us to cease fire, but it took quite some time for the firing to stop as we were really enjoying blazing away with live ammunition. When the noise of shooting died away, the snow storm had passed over and there was the Brigadier's caravan with its red flag to cease fire flying on top. As we were ordered to our feet we were told that the exercise had been called off because it seemed, whether by accident or design was not known, that the caravan had come under heavy fire at the height of the storm.

Since the exercise finished early it appeared that our transport, to take us back to camp, would be some time before it arrived, but rather than wait around we could make our own way back in sections by following the tracks that ran along the edge of the loch, if we wished. Our section decided to march back and off we set, by now soaked to the skin with sea water, snow and rain. Our way lay through rough narrow tracks with deep ruts, and acting like boys, we deliberately splashed our way through the rain-filled ruts, laughing and joking, arguing that we couldn't get much wetter, knowing that back in camp we could strip off, get into dry warm clothes and have a good hot meal.

But now we were soaking wet with no hope of drying ourselves off as the guards began to jostle us into position, and we realised why there had been so much commotion and recounting the previous night. Our guards had been changed. The Germans who had marched alongside our column from way back at the sugar factory had been replaced. The new ones, although not particularly smartly dressed, looked a lot fitter than their predecessors who by now seemed positively worn out with quite a few of them limping painfully. It looked as if they were going to have a rest from marching but we were going to be pushed along as usual, seemingly, until we reached the end of our tether.

We were lined up in threes to the satisfaction of the new men and the endless counting and recounting began again. This went on for so long that the sun was quite high in the sky before we were on the march again, with the guards showing their keenness and freshness by keeping us closed up tight in the column and not afraid to use their rifle butts on occasion.

For about a week we had been aware of a mountain range ahead of us in the distance. This was particularly noticeable because for most of our journey so far the countryside had been flat. The town where we spent the night in the flooded tennis court lay at the foot of these mountains and as soon as we set out that morning the road began to climb steeply. It was quite a nice day, fresh and springlike. The thunderstorm seemed to have washed the sky clean of the dirty dull greyness which had haunted us for most of the journey.

The road was quite narrow, so that the guards who escorted us on either side of the column forced us together. It didn't pay to jostle them for fear of a clout with a rifle butt, and they kept us very much shoulder to shoulder. The Germans who formed a semi-circle at the rear forced everyone tighter and tighter together so that we were practically walking on one another's heels.

The sun was shining and there was very litle wind. Soon, with the steepness of the climb and the saturated condition of our clothes and bodies we began to dry out. From our jammed-together marching, steam began to rise as we laboured upwards. We must have looked like a herd of cows going in for milking after a wet day in the fields, with steam rising off them as they bunch together in a narrow country lane. After a few miles the surface of the road became cobbled and we funnelled into a very narrow lane between a row either side of whitewashed cottages. They were long terraces of low buildings with their front doors opening directly onto the road which forced the guards to squash us together even more. Jammed together tightly, as we animals stumbled along the cobbled lane, a miasma formed above us and seemed to float in the air a couple of feet above the column. It was something like the small cloud of steam that forms above a scrum on a wet muddy day during an international match at Cardiff Arms Park, although that would smell a lot sweeter, and instead of not being able to tell the colour of the jerseys because of black mud, we were indistinguishable because of red mud, though by now the stuff had caked on our hands, feet and hair. It was only our clothes which were still sodden.

As we filed up the lane between the houses the front doors opened and women appeared to see what was going on. Most of them were very young and they seemed to be flabbergasted by the sight which met their eyes. Some of them rushed back inside and reappeared with jugs of milk which they began to offer to us.

This drove the guards into a frenzy. They roughly pushed the women back inside the doorways and pushed us on as if they didn't want anyone to see what they were escorting. We three were some way down the column and as we made our way between the houses we could see that the women were standing helplessly in their doorways holding their jugs of milk. Quite a lot of them were crying openly, so we must have looked a very sorry sight indeed.

The new guards were vicious to say the least, a vast change from the old ones who had acquired the knack of keeping themselves almost unnoticeable. With them we had slowly declined, so that we rambled along as if going into oblivion. If we had carried on long enough we would have dropped out one by one until nobody was left. But the old guards had some sort of feeling for us. Even that morning as we left the tennis court they had stood around in the dawn light and watched us getting ready to depart in our sodden condition as if they had some responsibility towards us.

We were all now in a really starving condition. I had landed in Normandy weighing about eleven stones and now I would have been lucky to make seven. Being pushed around by the replacement guards had an ill effect on us and everyone began to look the worse for wear. It was the worst thing that could have happened to us, to have a change of regime when we were plumbing the depths of our physical strength, a weakness which had slowly crept up on us almost without our noticing as we had rambled along the deserted roads.

We came out of the narrow lane between the houses and kept climbing up the road towards the top of the mountain, finding it very hard going indeed. At last the way became less steep and we came out onto a sort of plateau which was quite treeless and exposed like the top of a South Wales mountain.

It reminded me of the time that I had set out alone to walk across the Brecon Beacons. I was on an NCO's course which took place at the barracks in Brecon, a venerable grey stone complex with a large barrack square surrounded by high stone walls, barrack blocks and officers' quarters. A group of us had travelled from an outside battalion by train the previous week, and had actually passed through my home town of Newport on the way. This gave rise to a most frustrating feeling which I still carried with me a week later and which probably gave rise to my rather irresponsible actions on the first Saturday at the barracks.

We were allowed out into town on a Saturday after lunch and two of us changed and made our way to the exit from the barracks. This was a small door alongside the large double wooden gates set in the thick high stone walls. To reach this door to the outside world there was a narrow alleyway with a small door set into the wall on the left hand side. This was where we booked out at a high, counter-like desk, usually manned by a sergeant. As well as entering your name in a book he would look you over to make sure you were properly dressed and smart enough to maintain the image of the regiment. This was reinforced by a large mirror in which you could check yourself out. When we arrived at the booking-out desk we found that the room was empty. Being well-disciplined, we waited around for someone to appear. We waited for quite some time and were joined by a group of men from the regular barracks staff off on weekend leave. They were worried that they might lose their buses and decided to forget about booking out and make their way into town. We hung around for a short while longer and then, following their actions, walked out of the gate.

As we made our way towards the middle of the small town along the wide, tree-lined street we realised that we were in a sort of no man's land as far as the army was concerned and that we would not be missed until first parade on Monday morning, because there was no NCO billeted in our barrack room to report our absence, there was no roll call of any description on a Sunday and our empty beds could mean that we were on weekend leave. Whether or not it was because of our disciplinary indoctrination I don't know, but at that time we always did one thing at a time with little thought for the consequences. Almost without discussing the matter we made our way to the small railway station where we found a train for Newport actually waiting in the station, which was the end of the line. We bought a single ticket each and climbed aboard, keeping ourselves well out of sight.

By the middle of the afternoon we were on our way, the almost deserted train slowly making its way down towards the coast, stopping at every small halt and station so that the journey seemed interminable. As the light began to fail we drew near to Newport and only then thought of what would happen at Newport station, which was always full of military police. They would demand to see our leave passes at the iron grille exit gates and that would not only be the end of our escapade, but would put us in big trouble. As we were puzzling over the problem the train stopped at a small station, Bassaleg, the last stop before Newport. We hurriedly got out to find ourselves on a deserted platform, no police anywhere in sight and we were within walking distance of home.

My partner lived in Cardiff and we made our way to the bridge over the River Ebbw in Bassaleg for him to get a bus. I stayed with him until it arrived, both of us leaning over the bridge parapet looking at the black waters of the river, black from the coal washing up the valley. We arranged to meet outside Newport station the following day, Sunday, in the early afternoon to make our way back to Brecon before lights out. His bus pulled out and I began the long walk to my home in the evening light.

The town buses did not run until late afternoon on a Sunday so again I had to make the journey on foot back to the railway station after an enjoyable night at home. I arrived at the station to find the whole place shut up and deserted because it appeared that there were no trains on a Sunday. This also meant, luckily for me, that there were no military police about. Outside the station was the bus station for buses going up the valleys, one of which had the sign "Tredegar" in its destination window. The bus was deserted, with no driver or conductor anywhere about. As I waited for my partner in crime to turn up I decided that that was the only way to go, up to the top of the valley. I waited a long time but there was no sign of my companion when the crew of the bus arrived. I asked them about transport to Brecon and they told me that I could probably get a connection from Tredegar to Merthyr, but after that they had no idea. So I got on board to be driven to a part of the country which was quite strange to me.

Tredegar on a Sunday afternoon in wartime was deserted, with the dust being whirled about by a slight breeze and not a soul about to make enquiries of, until the bus for Merthyr turned up and carried me along the heads of the valleys. We were well on our way before the conductor came for my fare and it was then, on asking him, that I found out that Merthyr was the end of the line and that there was no service to Brecon on Sundays. I sat musing on this fact for a while and then decided that, having got so far, the only thing to do was to walk across the top of the Beacons, a distance of about fifteen miles. It was a route I knew because I had travelled it in an army lorry, and it was going to be a fine evening.

Having made my decision I asked the conductor to drop me off at the junction of the Brecon road and to point me in the right direction. It was uphill almost from the word go and, having decided to walk, the only thing to do was to push on as hard as I could and try to get back into the barracks before the gates were closed. To start with, there were houses on both sides of me, but these soon thinned out and I began to move through a deserted landscape, going higher and higher. I was now beginning to get seriously worried about whether I would get back into the barracks on time. After a while the going became a little easier with the road sloping away more gently in front of me. I passed a long narrow reservoir. The scenery was quite pleasant and I was enjoying the walk even when the mountain sides became bare and exposed.

I was about halfway across, and still worrying about the time, when I heard the sound of a vehicle coming up behind me. Turning round, I was amazed to see a small car making its way across the mountain in the same direction as me. As I stood at the side of the road, in the middle of nowhere, it pulled up beside me. In the car was a woman driver with another soldier beside her. He got out and let me squeeze into the narrow back seat. She told me that I was very lucky to get a lift from her because she only came that way once a month to see her mother in Merthyr, what with petrol rationing, and that she had never seen another vehicle on the road on a Sunday since the start of the war. I was effusive in my thanks as we bowled along over the top of the mountains and then down the long winding slope into the outskirts of Brecon itself, in no time at all.

Now that my worries about the time were over, I started to think about how I would get back into the barrack building without having to explain why my name wasn't in the book. I thought that it would be best to wait until after dark. Thanking the lady profusely, I got out of the car and made my way into the centre of Brecon, looking for comrades from the same course as myself. I found a group of them in one of the town's canteens. I explained my problem to them and they enthusiastically agreed to help me, so when it was dark the whole group of us made our way back to the small gate set in the barrack wall.

I suppose that I could have approached the sergeant on duty and told him that when I had gone out there was no-one at the desk, and got away with a good mouthful of abuse, but you could never tell with the army and I thought it was a much better idea to fiddle myself back in. After all, being absent without leave was a serious offence, and I didn't fancy twenty-eight days of sheer misery in a military prison. So the eight of us crowded into the narrow alleyway. A couple of us moved into the booking-in room, came out and stood outside as if waiting for the others, who jostled their way to face the sergeant on duty until there was quite a mix-up. I slipped past the open door and joined the waiting group. The sergeant gathered that there was something afoot and was looking around to find out what it was, but by that time I had moved on into the barrack square. I was home and dry.

But I certainly wasn't home and dry as we struggled over the German mountain. The day was fine, but with a bit of a wind, and we shivered with cold as the mountain air found its way through our threadbare clothes which were still wet. As we made our way across the mountain top we came across a group of German civilians who were cutting blocks of ice from a gully, wrapping them in sacks and putting them into a horse-drawn cart. We must have looked an unusual sight as we passed by them on the open mountain, but they didn't spare us a second glance. Maybe sights like us were becoming commonplace in Germany at that time.

We had set out much later than usual that morning and we kept on marching over the mountain and onto the down slope without a break, which was fine for the guards in their fit condition but murder for us. The only good thing was that the heat of our bodies slowly dried out our clothes. We kept going until long after dark and the night air was bitterly cold. Eventually in the middle of nowhere we were pushed into a hut with a concrete floor. It was as cold inside as it was out, so that very few people slept at all and we were glad to line up in the early morning for our fifth of a loaf. I gobbled mine down, which would have to do me until the next morning, provided we had another issue which wasn't at all certain. We had somehow given up hope that we would ever again have anything worthwhile to eat and just accepted whatever came along, which was barely enough to keep us alive. It seemed that only spiritual emotions kept us going, particularly the comradeship between the three of us. The discomfort of the concrete floored hut brought it home to us how lucky we had been sleeping in straw-filled barns. It looked as if we would find it hard going with the new guards if the sleeping quarters of the first two nights were anything to go by.

We carried on marching down the mountain that day and onto flat countryside into quite a well-inhabited part of the country. It was well into March by now. The weather was quite spring-like so that we could see what was going on around us as we carried on with our usual fifteen miles a day. At one point we passed an aerodrome with fighter planes taking off and landing without any hindrance. We had no idea how the war was going on, and the way life around us looked so normal, it didn't seem that anything much was happening on the front.

Another time we passed a factory which was working normally with smoke coming out of its chimneys. The building was in an isolated position, quite large, without any other buildings about. What was peculiar was the number of bomb craters in the flat countryside around. There were literally hundreds and hundreds of holes in the ground, so many that they even overlapped one another. Yet there was the factory working away, admittedly looking somewhat patched up. I wondered whether all the effort which had gone into bombing Germany was really worthwhile, particularly with the heavy loss of life among the aircrews.

This evidence of heavy bombing made us aware that the war was really still on. It was the first time that we had seen signs of hostilities since we left Normandy. Suddenly the drone of aeroplanes filled the air and up in the clear blue sky we could see what looked like a shoal of silver fish flying overhead. It was an American daylight raid, most impressive as the regimented lines of planes flew steadily over in strict formation. They went out of sight and shortly afterwards the ground beneath our feet began to shake. We heard no noise of bombs bursting so the raid must have been some distance away, and yet the explosions were fierce enough to vibrate the ground beneath our feet.

Looking behind, we could see that the mountain range which had been ahead of us a week previously was now well behind and beginning to fade into the distance. This gave us some idea of the distances we were being forced to travel. It seemed that there was going to be no letup as the guards kept us moving along at a rate of fifteen miles a day, with our physical condition worsening all the time.

Chapter eleven

Then one day the road surface became cobbled and we were shuffling along the gutters of the outer suburbs of Hanover. It was early in the morning and civilians walked past us on the pavements with the inevitable briefcases, going off to work without giving us a second glance. As we stumbled along the area became more built up and the occasional electric tram would pass us, running on metal tracks along the cobbled roads. After a few miles we turned off the main road to find ourselves at the gates of a factory built of red brick. We were herded across the factory yard and off to one side where we stopped outside a long wooden hut. The hut was barricaded all round with barbed wire fences, more barbed wire than I had ever seen before anywhere. The gates in the fence were opened, we were pushed inside and left to our own devices. It was hope that we might get food somewhere which kept us going, and with this hope we went into the hut to explore. But as ever there was nothing but a bare wooden floor. It was very gloomy inside because the few windows had all been painted over black as an air raid precaution. There was very little light inside except for a few chinks which came from between the door and the frame. It was quite a nice day, so rather than stay inside such an unpleasant place we made our way outside to sit in a long line with our backs against the wall of the hut with the spring sun in our faces. Sheltered from the wind, we sat and looked out of the compound and down the back gardens of a row of houses.

It was quite warm in the sun and then, quite casually, one of us absent-mindedly scratched under his armpit. As he did so the person next to him scratched as well, then the next person in the line and soon we were all scratching away until it dawned on us that there was something wrong. Feverishly we tore our clothes off to sit stripped to the waist. For the first time in almost three months we had taken our clothes off only to find that we were crawling with lice, every one of us. Our clothes were infested, and having disposed of the obviously visible ones, someone said that lice tended to live under the seams of clothes. Sure enough, turning back the seams of my undervest I saw them, hundreds of them, lying head to tail like grains of long, semi-transparent white rice with a pinkish dot in the middle. The only way of getting rid of them was to crack them between thumb and finger-nail. We sat for hours destroying as many as we could until the sun went in and a cold wind blew up.

With a feeling of revulsion I put my clothes back on, knowing full well that I was nowhere near clear of the disgusting creatures, and we went back into the hut to settle down for the night. The three of us huddled together on the bare floor in an effort to keep warm. As our bodies warmed up we became aware of the lice moving about on our skin, a horrible sensation, and we got very little sleep that night. What was annoying was that we had obviously been infested for some time but had been unaware of it. Once we had actually seen them lying head to tail in the seams of our clothes, then any irritation made us scratch away like mad.

The Germans had seen us delousing ourselves and the next morning, after our issue of a mouldy loaf between five, small groups of us were escorted across the factory forecourt to a shower block. There we were given a piece of ersatz soap, a thin tablet of highly perfumed greyish-green material which was better then nothing although it produced very little lather. This was the first wash which we had had since leaving the sugar factory back in December. A hot shower should have been a good occasion but by now we were becoming so half-starved that we could not whip up any enthusiasm for anything except food. As we stood under the hot water we looked at one another to see that our bodies had taken on a peculiar shape. The top half was emaciated, with sunken chests and shoulders like coathangers, yet from the waist down we were grotesquely swollen and mis-shapen, I suppose as a combined result of malnutrition and all the walking.

As we looked more closely at each other the people nearest to each other moved away and kept their distance as we saw grey movement on people's bodies as the heat of the water brought the lice to life. On some people there were what appeared to be "herds" moving about in patches, particularly on their backs. Finishing the shower, we dried ourselves with our shirts, got dressed and prepared to move back to the compound. We should have felt better in ourselves after the shower but putting back on clothes which we knew to be infested rather destroyed the effect. I was still wearing my old overcoat and French forage cap. Wherever I went or whatever I did, I never took them off. They were like a second skin to me because I couldn't forget the bitterly cold weather we had been through.

As we straggled back across the factory forecourt we passed a red brick building. A door opened at the top of a small flight of concrete steps outside the building and a woman appeared. She was a fat German woman wearing an apron and she was carrying a bucket of potato peelings which she tipped into an open trough against the wall at the foot of the steps without taking the slightest notice of us, as if she had seen it all before, which she probably had, because I should imagine that every factory and farm in Germany had its wooden hut surrounded with barbed wire where the slave labour was housed. It was a nation kept going with slaves like Caesar's Rome.

My self-respect had completely deserted me and along with a couple of others I leaned over the wall of the trough and began grovelling among the peelings for some thicker pieces to give me something to chew on. The peelings were very thin and mixed up with rotten cabbage leaves which had been there for some time and were very smelly and slimy. I managed to grab a handful of peelings before the guards moved in on me angrily, but even in my starved condition I could not stomach them and I threw them away.

Later that day we were called out on parade and lined up against the barbed wire fence in a single line, whereupon a German army doctor began to look at each one of us in turn. He was accompanied by a guard who would take notes from time to time. Thinking that there might be food somewhere we all tried to look as ill as possible, which wasn't very difficult. When the doctor got to us he pointed me out but left George and Busty alone. After the doctor had gone the guard dismissed the parade except for the marked individuals and told us that we would be moving on the next day. Another night of itching went by and then we formed up outside the factory and set off again with me waving goodbye.

It appeared that we were going to the main railway station in Hanover which was a few miles away. We had not gone far when evidence of the bombing raids began to become apparent and the further we went the worse it became. The road became a winding track through mounds of rubble with stark pieces of building sticking up. The track must have been quite a wide thoroughfare in its day, but now all the buildings on either side were completely destroyed. All the side roads were blocked off by mounds of rubble or some sort of loose brick rebuilt walls, though why anyone would want to go into such devastation I can't imagine. As far as I could see, the centre of the city had been totally destroyed with no-one living in the area at all. It was like moving through a lunar landscape until we arrived at the station which was, surprisingly, full of people waiting to catch trains. We were stood on the platform for a while and were then pushed into a corner out of sight as if we offended the nostrils of the German travellers. I could see to my surprise that most of the station buildings were intact but the roof, which was made of lattice ironwork, was completely devoid of glass. The tracks were still in place and obviously in use, although I saw no trains that day.

We had come through the ruins at a leisurely pace, shambling along, partly because the roadway was so narrow but mainly because of the very poor condition of some of us. During the winter march we had been joined by four or five South Africans, much older than us, and they were in a very bad way. One had to be supported by his friends on the way to the station, but it appeared that even this had been too much for him and he collapsed on the ground with his friends anxiously watching over him.

We hung around the station all day but there was no sign of any transport. Eventually as darkness fell, we gathered that we had to make the journey back to the compound. It was obvious that the sick South African could not make it on his own feet, and the rest of us were too weak to carry him. His friends, being Afrikaans-speaking, were able to communicate with the guards quite easily, while I personally had not exchanged one single word with the guards since I had been taken. The result of their conversation was that they went off and returned with a flat-topped two-wheeled cart on which they laid their sick companion. Off we set on the road back to camp with the South

Africans wheeling their cart along in the middle of us. It got very dark as we went along on our weird journey, stumbling over loose bricks in our path through the mounds of rubble. It took us several hours to get back to a dead quiet hut with everybody asleep. The counting and recounting of our little group, which took place just inside the compound, was carried out in much quieter voices than usual. The reason for this, I learned, was that the South African had quietly passed away on the return journey.

I spent the night huddled up with George and Busty. The next morning, saying goodbye to them again, I fell in outside the compound and set off again through the ruined city to the station. On arriving there we were kept hanging about just as on the previous day. Then we were marched down onto the track, given a long-handled shovel and told to tidy up the ballast between the lines. The ballast was new and the sleepers had just been put into position so it looked as if the track had been bombed quite recently. Giving me a shovel was a bit of a joke. I hardly had the strength to lift it up and could just about scratch at the small stones. Luckily the guards were only going through the motions and we spent the afternoon without anyone bothering us as we half pretended to do some work. Even this did me no good and I began to feel terrible, as if I didn't have long to live, and I realised what a mistake I had made in leaving George and Busty. When I was with them I had never felt so beaten.

No trains ran again that day but as night fell we did not head back to the compound but were escorted to a windowless concrete building alongside the railway track quite near the station. The door was opened and we were shoved inside. The door stayed open long enough for us to see that the windowless room had about three feet of dirty, damp compacted straw filling its interior except where it sloped up from the doorway. In the dim light we picked our spots and lay down. The door slammed shut and we heard the guards lock it.

I had definitely made a big mistake leaving my two friends. I lay with my head against one of the walls in complete darkness and solitude and contemplated my position. My first worry was what my chances would be if there were an air raid because we were right in the middle of Hanover and I had seen what the rest of the city was like.

As I lay there one of the worst moments of my life happened. The filthy straw began to move. With the warmth of our bodies giving some increase in temperature the straw actually became alive. It rustled and then became increasingly noisy as the fleas, cockroaches and God knows what else slithered around us in the pitch dark. I hurriedly got to my feet and stood unsteadily in the straw with my back against the wall, and that is how I spent the night. The fact that I knew that I was already infested with lice didn't help matters either, and having actually seen them in my clothes made my imagination run riot as I thought of how many millions of the horrible creatures there could be in such a mass of straw. It was the worst night of my life.

Early the next morning, thankfully, we were released from that awful place and taken across to a station platform where a train was already standing. With one guard we were herded on board and in company with German civilians and army personnel we were given seats in an ordinary compartment. The seats were made of wood and were a vast improvement on the usual cattle truck. The train soon set off and after quite a long journey we were disembarked and set to shambling along a road to a large prisoner of war camp complete with double barbed wire fences, watch towers and a host of guards. After several counts and recounts the gates were opened and we were left to wander inside the camp.

The camp was divided into separate sections for each nationality of prisoner. Our section was populated mainly by paratroopers captured at Arnhem, but now the camp was becoming overcrowded with small groups coming in from all over Germany. I wandered around until I found a vacant spot in a hut where I could lie down and consider my fate. I had left George and Busty behind, thinking that I could get to a better situation, but there was nothing in this place for me and I didn't even have their companionship to help keep up my morale. As the days went by I became quite apathetic. I just lay about in the hut and could see myself passing away peacefully with no-one even realising that I had gone. My only trips outside were to the latrines because like everyone else in the overcrowded conditions I was suffering from a severe form of looseness of the bowels which took the form of terrific pains in the stomach and resulted in a mad dash for the latrines.

These were situated in a hollow, and would have been adequate for the original population of the camp, but proved totally inadequate for the large numbers which were now using them, most of the time in a great hurry. First the toilet pans filled up because the flushing water couldn't keep up with the usage, then people began to use the floor until a six-inch layer of excrement covered it completely and began to flow out of the door. Then the area outside the building was used, and slowly a semi-circle of excrement grew outwards. This was very hazardous, particularly if one was taken short in the middle of the night, because you never really knew how far the semicircle had reached and with the speed it was growing you could easily step into a layer deep enough to come over the top of your boots. This situation didn't help me at all as I became more and more withdrawn. The latrine problem was eventually solved by digging deep ditches with a long log to sit on. These logs were never empty and one usually had to queue up, desperately trying to control oneself. With the new trenches the awful stench which hung over the camp subsided a little.

Then one day it appeared that we had been liberated. By then I felt so withdrawn that it meant almost nothing to me. There had been no noise of battle or anything to indicate that release was at hand so I continued to shamble about. A few of us ventured out of the gates and into the countryside. We wandered about until we came to a large farmhouse. Someone suggested that we should ask for eggs and butter so we went to the open door and banged on it. After a long time an old woman came out and we managed by sign language to show her what we wanted. She went back inside and we waited in a circle around the door for her return, half-starved, filthy, lousy, in threadbare clothes and worn out boots which were now tied together with string from Red Cross parcels. She came back with about a dozen eggs and a pat of butter. We grabbed them and wandered on our way until we came to a little dell where we lit a fire, crouched down and fried the eggs in the butter on an aluminium plate which one of us was carrying. We gobbled them down and they tasted marvellous to our deprived palates, but we had made a big mistake because our stomachs refused to accept such rich food after such a long time, and in no time at all we were dropping our trousers in a great hurry.

So we wended our way back to camp feeling a lot weaker than we left, determined to eat as little as possible for the time being. The camp was laid out on the side of quite a steep hill and on the skyline above the camp huts was a series of large concrete buildings which looked as if they were barracks, but were in fact warehouses stuffed with all sorts of goods.

One section of the camp was occupied by Italians, a large number of them, and the outer barbed wire fence of their compound was immediately below the warehouses. On our return to camp an amazing sight met our eyes. The Italians had broken through the fence and into the warehouses to find that one of them was full of paper sacks of macaroni. There they were, two long lines of ant-like creatures, one line struggling up the slope to the warehouse and the other coming down in the opposite direction with each man carrying a large paper sack of macaroni on his back, as if they were laying up supplies for years to come.

A large crowd of British prisoners was standing about, most of them with a smile on their faces because it was an amusing sight and for the first time in months I managed to raise a smile. What tickled me was that I felt no need for food in any quantity knowing that I could have more or less what I wanted, but the Italians clearly thought that their days of hardship weren't yet over. We decided to have a stroll up to the warehouses to see what was going on . We went into one, a large cavernous place full of every manner of goods and with no-one about to stop us we rifled through the various stacks. As a souvenir I picked up a small cardboard box which I found contained six bottles of 4711 Eau-de-Cologne and then went back to the camp. Lying there in the dark I thought that I would go back to the warehouse in the morning to see what else I could pick up, but it was not to be, because suddenly the skyline was lit up by a red glare. We went outside to find that someone had set fire to the buildings and they were well ablaze.

The next morning they were still smouldering away when army lorries arrived at the camp and started to take people away. I clambered aboard one and rode for quite a long way through war-torn Germany. The roads were strewn with debris and we passed buildings which were shell-torn or simply piles of rubble. We arrived at an aerodrome which was even more badly damaged than some of the buildings we had seen, but nevertheless the runway had been patched up and there waiting for us was a row of Dakota aircraft. In no time at all we shuffled into lines and got aboard to take off almost immediately. The aircraft had blacked-out windows with bucket seats each side of the fuselage so that we sat facing one another across an aisle. Opposite me were all sorts of nationalities from the British Empire, all colours and creeds who, like me, had probably not flown before. As we crossed the English Channel the plane met quite nasty turbulence, dropping sharply at one point, so that my already-queasy stomach felt as if it were going to fall out of me, while the people opposite looked terrified. Although we had been free for a few days I still hadn't washed or tidied myself up, for one thing we had no facilities. I was still wearing my French forage cap and overcoat which I hardly ever took off, it was part of me, and I was still infested with lice which I had done nothing about since the day we had sat in the sun outside the wooden hut in Hanover, mainly because I had almost given up the ghost as I became more and more withdrawn.

The plane landed in Southern England, the door was opened and there to greet us was a line of girls from the Women's Royal Air Force dressed in immaculate blue uniforms with clean, shining faces. As we got out, one of the girls took each of us over to a large building. The girl escorting me took me by the arm. I must have looked pretty awful but I shook her off and explained to her that I was lousy and that she should keep her distance.

Inside, the building was very well organised to deal with returning prisoners. First I undressed completely and kicked my lousy clothes into a pile destined for burning. It was almost like a snake sloughing its skin, particularly the French overcoat to which I had become very attached. Next I was shown into a row of showers streaming with hot water, with large bars of soap which actually lathered. Then I was given a large white bath towel to dry myself on. I couldn't believe that such luxury still existed. Stark naked, I walked out of the shower into a room where facing me was a line of desks occupied by RAF personnel including doctors, one of whom was a female which gave me rather a shock. Unabashed, I answered a lot of questions. I was asked whether I had been wounded and when I answered yes, and showed where, I was given a thorough examination for which I was quite grateful because it was the first time any medical person had looked at my wound. I hoped that the doctor wouldn't find anything wrong because if he did I might not get away home. He seemed satisfied and when I said that it wasn't giving me any trouble that was the end of the matter and the whole incident became just an entry in a form.

After the medical examination I moved along to be questioned about the sort of treatment I had received at the hands of the Germans. The RAF officers wanted to know if I had been ill-treated, or had been the victim of any atrocities. I wasn't quite sure what they meant, to my way of thinking the whole of my captivity had been one long example of ill-treatment, but I wasn't in any frame of mind to go into detailed explanations of what had happened to me, the continuous lack of food and the march across Germany in winter. Only that morning I had been in a Stalag, my mind was confused and I found it difficult to concentrate. I wanted to get home and out of it as soon as possible, so I mumbled something about it not being too bad and they let me go on my way.

I was let loose into a quartermaster's stores to be fitted out with new clothes and boots. In the meantime I had nipped back to the arrival point to pick up my little cardboard box with its bottles of Eau-de-Cologne which I had left behind while I showered, and so I walked naked into the clothes store just carrying my little box as the only thing I had left to remind me of my travels.

As I left the medical inspection area I was struck by how clean and healthy everybody looked, much better than any of the Germans I had come into contact with, and it began to dawn on me that I was back in the land of the living. Before I entered the clothes store I was liberally doused with delousing powder which was something I was very much in need of, and then got dressed in my new underclothes, shirt, socks, battledress and boots which felt most peculiar after my pulp-like footwear held together with Red Cross parcel string.

This was the first time that I had been kitted out with all brand new clothing since my first days in the army. Some kind soul had ensured that the quality of the clothing was much better than that normally issued to a footsoldier. The trousers and jacket matched perfectly and were in the dark green of a Canadian uniform. The trousers were much too long so that I had to tuck them into my new long white woollen socks. I had never had such luxurious socks before and I was glad to show them off, because I wasn't given any webbing gaiters to wrap around my ankles.

The new clothing made me feel a lot better in myself and tended to mask my emaciated frame so that I was ready for the journey home. I was then given spare clothing which I put into a new kitbag. I was then showed into a lorry to join a small group of ex-paratroop prisoners and we travelled to a large detached house just outside London.

Here there were civilian women who took my battledress jacket and sewed my regimental insignia on. I was given a long-overdue haircut, filled in various forms and then sat about while the day wore on. I was then given the opportunity to send a telegram to my family to let them know that I would be home the next day, and this was the best thing that had happened to me since I was liberated. It really brought home to me the fact that the nightmare was over, although I couldn't shake off the effects so quickly. Actually to know, and to be telling someone, what I would be doing the next day, began to break down the feelings of hopelessness which had enveloped me during the last few weeks of my captivity. But I was still in the same frame of mind as in the prisoner of war camp that same morning. I was still feeling very anti-social and withdrawn and I sat all alone on a wooden seat in the suburban garden feeling very sorry for myself until it was time to go to sleep.

The next morning I got up early, had a very small breakfast because my stomach was still in a very agitated state, and lined up with a few others to get my new pay book, some money, and a rail warrant for South Wales. I was also issued with several hundred cigarettes which helped to fill my kitbag a little. I had a leave pass for seven weeks - seven whole weeks before I had to report back for duty. Then outside to another army lorry which took me right into London and dropped me off at Paddington Station.

The train for South Wales was already at the platform and when I got on I found that it was already full, as trains normally seemed to be in wartime. I made my way along the corridor for the length of the train but to no avail. I stopped outside a compartment full of middle aged women who looked as if they had been on a shopping trip to London, hoping that they would squash up and offer me a seat, but there was no response to my questioning glance. So I put my kit bag down and sat on it with my back against the sliding door of the compartment. It was a sunny April afternoon as the train clattered along through the green English countryside. As it rattled along my bony back bumped against the door and I began to feel even more sorry for myself.

With the compartment door open I could clearly hear the valley accents of the plump women. After a while the woman nearest the door, noticing I suppose that I was looking most uncomfortable, and probably nosey like most women from South Wales, poked her head around the open door and said in her singsong voice,
"And where have you come from?"
to which I replied in a soulful voice,
"I've been a prisoner of war".
Mulling this over in her mind for a while, during which time I thought they might make room for me, she suddenly said,
"Well, you don't look too bad on it".
I knew I was nearly home.

Epilogue

Some twenty years after the war I went back to Normandy for a week's holiday at Easter time. It was a motoring holiday for four of us, my wife, myself, a friend of mine and his wife. He had been in the same regiment as myself but a different battalion, and had also fought in Normandy, mainly at Hill 112. He still had vivid memories of the terrible loss of life of thousands of British and German infantrymen.

We sailed from Southampton to Cherbourg with my new dark green de luxe Triumph Herald, proudly displaying our brand new GB sign. After some small problems with driving on the right, particularly at the first roundabout we encountered as we left the dockyard, we set out along the Normandy coast, intending to get bed and breakfast accommodation wherever convenient.

We drove along until we came to the British invasion beaches and there among the sand dunes we had a picnic and a drink from our duty free bottles. It was quite a pleasant day as we lay back in the sand with only the sound of seabirds breaking the silence of the completely deserted beach, only spoilt by my friend. He had brought a new camera with him which he handed to his wife who, bubbling with laughter, was busy snapping him paddling out of the sea waving a piece of stick to which he had attached a white handkerchief, just to remind me of my short stay in Normandy the last time I had been there. Time was getting on and we had made no arrangements for the night so we made our way to a small seaside town to try to find accommodation. We had the greatest difficulty getting in anywhere because it was a Bank holiday weekend and all the hotels were full. We drove around for a long time and finally as darkness fell we got fixed up in a small town some way inland in a not very salubrious bar with the four of us sleeping in the same room on two narrow beds.

Needless to say we woke up early, had breakfast in a nearby cafe and were on our way back to the coast. We went to Arromanches to have a look at the Invasion museum and the guns and vehicles surrounding it. We then drove quietly along the coast looking at a map of the area, stopping to look at places of interest until we came to an area which I thought was perhaps where I had come ashore. We decided to make our way to Bayeux by striking straight inland until we came to the Caen–Bayeux road. This suited me well, although I said nothing, because I was hoping very much that we might find the farmhouse where my problems had begun.

After we had driven for quite a few miles I vaguely began to associate my surroundings with my half-forgotten memories. We went through a small village with a high wall on our left hand side and it seemed to me that it was the same place that we had marched through in sections in single file, hugging the wall as our tanks also made their way along the narrow lane. Telephone wires were down and hanging in the roadway and as the tanks passed the loose wires were caught up in their tracks, pulled taut and then snapped with twanging noises as they whipped about. We had moved along very quickly without any need for encouragement. It was the sort of place not easily forgotten and I was quite hopeful that we were in the right area.

After the village came more definite evidence because we drove across a level crossing over a railway line. After the lane with the telephone wires down, we had moved forward, finally taking cover in a hamlet of shell-damaged buildings which were still blazing, and there we had stayed until dark. When it was completely black we fell in on the road, moved forward for a few miles across a railway line and turned left, along a sunken lane.

Having moved around in total darkness all those years ago I was not quite sure where to go after crossing the railway line. I felt a strange tugging and at the next turning almost unconsciously turned left into a lane. We drove along the narrow lane with its thick high hedges on both sides, with no idea of where we were heading until we joined another lane and then I knew that I had found the place. The lane turned sharp right at this point but the way continued on into a grassy lane and I pulled into it. Quietly I got out of the car. There on the left was the railway line. On my right was the ditch I had crawled down, with the farmhouse at the end of the field, and the hedge behind which

I had taken cover and where my friend's blood had stained the ground.

I stood there for a moment feeling that something strange had drawn me to the exact spot, the place where so many of my fellow footsoldiers had been killed, men from the South Wales valleys who had not been so fortunate as myself in getting back home eventually. It could well have been my imagination but I definitely felt a strange feeling in the air, a feeling accompanied by knowing somehow that someone was very glad to see me.

The moment was soon lost as the others got out of the car, finding it hard to believe that I had actually got back to the place which they had heard so much about. We strolled up the grassy lane past the entrance to the field through which my German captor had directed me, turned round and took a few photographs. When these photographs were developed they looked very ordinary and could have been a field, a ditch or a farmhouse anywhere. It was the normal everyday look of the area which got to me, and I began to feel a quiet peace inside. For many years I had had quite nasty dreams about my experiences but I now knew that most of this effect was over.

My fellow travellers were in a hurry to get along to Bayeux so we got back into the car, reversed into the lane and drove down alongside the ditch. We then turned left and stopped outside the front gate of the farmyard which was facing the front of the house, which this time had its front door closed. We got out of the car again. This was a new experience, viewing the farmyard from a different angle, but still looking very much the same with its rows of rabbit hutches lining the walls.

While we were leaning on the gate, me with my mind full of mixed memories, my friend said to me that I should go and knock on the front door. When I asked him why he said that probably someone would come to the door, throw their hands in the air and say,
"Where on earth have you been, Haden, your tea's getting cold!"

